The Little Book of Big Healing

INTRODUCING THE EASE IN METHOD FOR SELF-HEALING BODY, MIND, AND SPIRIT

By Joey Lott

www.joeylott.com

ISBN: 9781703096231

Table of Contents

How to Read This Book

Dear Reader,

This truly is a little book of big healing. I will share with you the exact process that I and others have used to find profound healing, allowing for the resolution of anxiety, chronic fatigue, anorexia, depression, self-hatred, OCD, chronic pain, and more.

Before we begin, however, I have a request of you. Yes, right from the start I am going to ask you for a favor.

Here it is: please be willing to read this book with an open mind. Don't close your mind. Don't reach conclusions.

Even when you find yourself agreeing, be willing to remain open to what is neither agreeing nor disagreeing. And when you disagree, be open to what is neither agreeing nor disagreeing.

This is the spirit in which I offer you this book. And I truly wish for you to receive it in this spirit. Because I believe that when you receive it in this spirit, we can meet here in this openness. And as you will discover through this book, this openness, this wholeness, is the source and essence of healing.

It is my observation from my flawed and incomplete perspective, that this world has enough conclusions to last for many generations. As someone I know used to say, "Everybody has an opinion...that and $1.75 will get you a latte at Starbucks." Of course, you'll need a lot more than $1.75 to get anything at Starbucks these days, but the point remains valid.

We can so easily form opinions. They are cheap. And do they really contribute value to our lives?

I suggest that there is another way. It is the way of not concluding, neither agreeing nor disagreeing. When we come together in this way, we can truly meet. And then perhaps we can discover something of value that enriches our lives.

I don't ask you to believe anything in this book. In fact, I prefer that you don't believe anything in this book because then I will only be giving you more baggage. From my perspective, we have more than enough baggage. I may make some bold claims in this book. But don't *believe* them. Just find out for yourself through investigating as I guide you to do. Then you don't need belief.

Many of us – maybe most of us – have been taught that if only we can accumulate more stuff – more knowledge, more experience, more wisdom, more practices, more techniques, more possessions – that will give us what we truly want – that will fulfill us.

Yet if we tell the truth, despite all the stuff, are we fulfilled? Are we happy? Do we recognize and appreciate the richness of our lives? Or are we just looking for the next fix, the next thing to patch up our dissatisfaction and loneliness and unhappiness?

My request is that you don't burden yourself with anything more. At least not from me. Not from this book. Perhaps you can view it as a game or a challenge: just see if you can receive this book as it comes and then just as quickly let it go. Like standing in a river allowing the water to rush over you. You needn't grasp it. To do so would be futile. But you can allow it to wash over you.

Feel free to let what is of value to you be of value to you without needing to cling to it. And feel free to let what seems valueless fall away without clinging. I am not perfect. I am not always right. And I cannot give you the perfectly packaged words and message that will be the one-size-fits-all remedy to all your discomfort. I can't solve all your problems or perceived problems.

But if you're willing, we can meet here in vulnerability and tenderness and discover together what can be discovered. And we can let that be enough. And we can let that sprout and blossom.

I might be wrong about some things. I might be right about some things. Who can know? And if we tell the truth about it, do we really want to know who is right and who is wrong? Or do we really want something simpler?

I believe we want something simpler. I believe we want this moment as it is. Despite all our fighting and clinging and protesting and arguing, I believe we just want this. And what I am sharing with you in this book is what I have found is a way to open to and live from this wonder and awe and humility. Not "perfectly" Not as a saint. Not as the perfectly enlightened sage. Not as a god.

Just as we are. Not knowing. Flawed. Greedy. Mistaken. And yet finding that is enough. All that we truly want.

This book is my prayer. May all discover what is most wonderful for them now and now and now. May this touch upon our hearts and minds and guide us to live well. This is the prayer of a fool. I accept that. It is my prayer all the same. I am willing to be myself: the fool.

Part I: Introduction

In this book I introduce you to what I call the Ease In Method. I call it the Ease In Method because it is a simple method that helps you to *ease in* to a recognition of wholeness and then to find *ease in* life. This is a process that you can use to find true healing, not just another empty promise of a quick fix.

What Are the Benefits of the Ease In Method

We live in a time in which we are promised instant gratification frequently. We are told that we can go from poverty to millions of dollars in under 30 days, develop an idealized physique in two weeks, and instantly manifest parking spaces and winning lottery tickets.

Not only that, we're often told that it will require no effort on our part. It will be without any discomfort. It will be entirely enjoyable.

If that's what you're looking for, this is not the book for you. Put it down now. Please don't continue reading. I will disappoint you entirely.

On the other hand, there are also many systems and philosophies that requiring great sacrifices now in which the benefits never seem to come.

The Ease In Method is not that either.

The Ease In Method offers real benefits that you can begin to experience right away and that also grow over time. It won't work if you expect that you can just flip a switch and have your life look the way you want it to without any commitment and investment on your part. But on the other hand, it doesn't require huge upfront investments of your time and energy without any benefits.

Now, since you're still reading, I can speak frankly with you. What can you honestly expect with the Ease In Method?

Since you are still reading, I can guess that you are someone who is at a point in your life when you are ready to be deeply honest with yourself. You've realized on some level that the other strategies you've used in your life to try to get rid of what you don't want and get what you do want haven't really satisfied you.

Maybe they've seemed to yield some results, but ultimately, they haven't given you what you most deeply want. You still feel that something is off. No matter how much or how little you have, it doesn't give you the lasting experience of freedom, wholeness, compassion, and connection that you most deeply long for.

It may be that your life is fairly good. Maybe you have health, loving relationships, money, and a sense of purpose in life. But still, something seems to be not enough or not quite right. Perhaps you've even had glimpses of wholeness, but that doesn't seem to translate into a life that expresses the attributes of that wholeness.

Or maybe, like was true for me ten years ago, you are at a point of desperation. Maybe you feel that you are at a dead end. Maybe you see clearly that nothing you've ever done trying to fix yourself or your life has worked. Maybe you can see that everything has only gotten worse from all your efforts.

Either way, the Ease In Method can help. It can help you because you are mature enough to apply it earnestly.

When you are humble enough – as you are because you are still reading this – to admit that your ways haven't ultimately fulfilled you, you can begin to make use of this approach.

The Ease In Method is the most direct approach I am aware of for discovering both deep, inner fulfillment and peace *and* the outer expression of that fulfillment and peace.

Many meditative approaches offer access to inner peace. Many manifestation teachings (such as the so-called Law of Attraction) offer a promise of outer expression of fulfillment (though I question how effective they are at offering true fulfillment). The Ease In Method bridges the gap and provides a fully integrated way to discover inner fulfillment *and* the outer expression of that fulfillment.

In other words, the Ease In Method is a direct process for the discovery and embodiment of true wholeness.

It is a method of what I consider to be true healing. Whereas most of us think of healing as being about recovery (covering over again) – fixing something that has gone wrong – I consider true healing to be the discovery (the uncovering) of wholeness. In fact, that is what the real meaning of the word "to heal" is – a restoration of (the recognition of already-present) wholeness.

By the practical application of the Ease In Method you will discover ever-present wholeness in your direct experience. Yet we don't stop there because that can become a subtle form of suffering when we settle for the "mere" inner experience of wholeness. With the Ease In Method we discover how this wholeness can move us and guide our actions so that we can express this wholeness in our lives. This means that we not only heal inwardly. We also heal outwardly. Our bodies, minds, relationships, our sense of purpose, and all aspects of ourselves heal. That is, they come into alignment with wholeness.

The basic premise is that wholeness is already the case. Your present direct experience is already of wholeness. You don't need to create wholeness. You don't need to seek for it. It is already here. And when you learn how to apply this simple method, I am confident that you'll find this for yourself. (Of course, I'm not asking that you believe me. You'll be able to discover for yourself if I'm right.)

If this is true, why do you not currently perceive wholeness? The simple answer is that you, like the majority of us, have been trained to filter your experience through a conceptual overlay. The conceptual overlay, while potentially useful, can deceive us into wrongly perceiving ourselves as separate and the universe as being "out there" and made of lots of separate things. When we believe that to be true, we mistakenly believe that what we are experiencing is not wholeness. Then we act from that belief and our outer expression seems to confirm our belief in separation and suffering. It is a vicious cycle.

But when we learn to ease in to the direct experience, we learn how to easily perceive what is without the conceptual filtering. We don't need to get rid of anything. We don't need to get rid of concepts or do battle with the conditioned mind. But we can ease in to the direct experience which is, in some sense, greater than the conceptual overlay. This lets us directly perceive wholeness that is always here.

That is the first step of the two steps of the Ease In Method.

The second step of the Ease In Method is to quietly allow this subtle direct experience of wholeness to move us and our actions so that we act in congruence with our deep, authentic desires. Our deep, authentic desires express through us and our lives in ways that are fulfilling and meaningful to us. They express that wholeness in ways that are much greater than our previous beliefs and agendas let on were possible.

None of this requires analysis. We don't need to do 10-step worksheets. We don't need to attend lots of seminars or learn complicated processes. Instead, through easing in to our direct experience, we can simply let wholeness move us. This may seem difficult to believe or understand now. But it will become clear with practice.

Which brings us to the next question: how long does this take to "work"?

It works both instantaneously and progressively.

I already suggested earlier that the Ease In Method is not like many of the instant gratification promises that we're so familiar with these days. So it might seem suspicious that I've just said that the benefits of the Ease In Method are (at least in part) instantaneous.

But it is true. It is true because the instant that we ease in to direct experience, we discover ever-present wholeness that is not dependent upon any conditions. This is always here and intimately available.

In Part II of this book I'll guide you into a series of explorations that will help you to ease in to direct experience so that you can discover this for yourself. You will find that you have access to ever-present wholeness at any time, no matter what the circumstances.

Easing into direct experience instantly dissolves all problems. You'll see this is true, so you don't need to believe me. I'll guide you to see this for yourself.

But typically, half a second later we again leap back to the conditioned, reactive mind and again the problems appear. When that happens, we might doubt whether there was any benefit at all.

Which is why the benefits are both instantaneous and progressive. Any time we ease in to direct experience, we discover ever-present wholeness and the instant disappearance of problems. But when we apply the second step of the Ease In Method and allow ourselves to be moved by wholeness to act in accordance with our authentic desires, we find that progressively, over time, our outer experience comes to better reflect the wholeness we have discovered inwardly. Or, better put, we cease to wrongly perceive separation; we start to see the wholeness is already expressing outwardly as well as inwardly. The seeming boundaries between inner and outer soften, and we start to find that our lives flow without so much effort.

But lest you think I'm selling you pie in the sky, let me qualify what I've just told you. Because these changes, this softening and flow and recognition of true wholeness that is both inner and outer requires humility and patience. It requires consistent, persistent application of the Ease In Method. I have not achieved some perfected state. I still have to apply the method. It just gets easier to do so because it is so rewarding.

In a world in which we are promised instant gratification, the notion that we might have to apply a method persistently in order to experience progressive benefits might not seem so appealing. Furthermore, so-called "direct path" spiritual philosophies often scoff at anything progressive. For those who have not yet developed the maturity to accept that true wholeness is inclusive and has room for *both* immediate, direct realization *and* progressive transformation, the Ease In Method may seem offensive. But my experience makes it clear to me that wholeness doesn't need to negate anything. All is included. We can instantly recognize wholeness and allow a progressive healing in our manifest lives.

Let me ground all of this in more practical terms. What specific kinds of benefits can you expect from the Ease In Method? I have personally used this method to heal from severe anxiety, obsessive-compulsive disorder, extreme sound sensitivity, chronic insomnia, chronic pain, dysfunctional relationship patterns, low self-esteem, chronic Lyme disease, anorexia, multiple chemical sensitivity, and body dysmorphic disorder. I've coached many people into using this method to heal from many of the same conditions as well as depression, post traumatic stress disorder, phobias, and more.

Although it may be difficult for you at this point to understand how one method could be so effective for such a diversity of troubles, with experience you will discover first hand that it truly is. We are "manifesting" all the time. While it may be true that we are each born into different circumstances that do have an impact on our experiences, it is also true that we allow our conditioning to determine our actions, which then generates more of the same kinds of experiences that confirm for us our conditioning. It becomes a vicious cycle that leads us to perceive ourselves as victims.

We have much more power than we typically believe. But that power is not *ours* in the sense that we possess it. Rather, that power is the power of wholeness. When we learn how to directly access wholeness and then allow that wholeness to move us into expressing our authentic desires, the limitations, obstacles, and problems we previously believed were real can dissolve.

Importantly, however, this is an "inner to outer" approach. If we start from the superficial, conditioned ideas of what we *think* we desire, we won't find true fulfillment. But when we allow ourselves to be moved from our authentic desires, we find true fulfillment, not only inwardly, but also outwardly.

Here's a simple example to illustrate what I mean. At a superficial level I might think that what I want is a million dollars. Will the Ease In Method give me a million dollars? Perhaps. But perhaps not. The Ease In Method is not about manifesting a million dollars for the sake of a having a million dollars.

What the Ease In Method does is lets us connect to our authentic desires arising from wholeness. These authentic desires are qualities of wholeness in expression. Things like love, life, freedom, okayness, connection, and peace. When we use the Ease In Method to move us from wholeness, our lives begin to reflect these qualities more clearly.

If having a million dollars is a true expression of an authentic desire, then we will manifest a million dollars. But not because having a million dollars is an authentic desire. A million dollars won't give fulfillment. The superficial desire for a million dollars is a distortion of a deeper, authentic desire. Ultimately, that desire doesn't need a name. It is an expression of a quality of wholeness.

When we are moved by wholeness, we discover that our lives reflect wholeness. We recognize that we are deeply fulfilled, and that shows up in expression in our lives. This is better than a million dollars.

Here's a simple example to illustrate this. I have known about the Ease In Method (though I didn't give it that name until recently) for seven years. I have been applying it in my life. And still, I have challenges – experiences that I perceive as being unpleasant or difficult or painful.

Does that mean that I'm doing it wrong? Not at all. Because my most authentic desire is not merely to have the ideal personal experiences every moment. My most authentic desire is to express wholeness, which has qualities such as compassion and humility. I desire to be able to connect with others and see their wholeness and beauty. And for me, part of that discovery involves being humbled by my own humanity and my own difficulties in life. Through my own experience of "imperfection" I get to discover my connection with others.

Perhaps some day I will be compassionate enough and humble enough that I will no longer need to be humbled by my own "imperfection". But for now, it is a gift that I gratefully accept. And the beauty of the Ease In Method is that in this moment, no matter what is happening, no matter what apparent difficulties I may experience, I have instant access to wholeness in which it is clear that there are no true problems. This offers instant healing as well as progressive healing. And this is what I will share with you to discover for yourself.

My Story of Discovering the Ease In Method

You don't need to know nor care about how the Ease In Method came about. But it is often helpful and inspirational for those new to this approach to know something of my story. Ultimately, my story isn't very important except in as much as it helps us to connect and helps to inspire you to apply this approach for yourself.

I grew up on the edges of rural and suburban southern Illinois. I lived with my parents, who were reasonably happily married, and my younger sister. I had aunts and uncles and cousins nearby. I had friends and did well in school. I had no serious illnesses. My father worked as an electrician for General Motors and we had a comfortable life.

In other word, I had a pretty good life. But having a pretty good life didn't immunize me against suffering. As I'll now share with you, my life began to look like a nightmare.

When I was in fourth grade one of my friends came up to me on the schoolyard, grabbed my nipple, and said some things that hurt worse than his rough handling of my body.

I was horrified. I had recently become aware that I had developed breasts. I knew this was not normal or expected for boys, so I felt uncomfortable about it. But his action led me to feel humiliated and I wanted to hide.

For the next few years I tried to dress myself in a way that would hide the shape of my chest. I preferred to wear thick, stiff shirts. I had only a few shirts that I felt really hid my chest, and I would wear those day after day.

When I was in seventh grade, my sister commented to my mom one day about how I frequently pulled at and adjusted my shirts when I wore them – a behavior I did compulsively in an attempt to hide my chest better. When she said that I felt more humiliated than ever. I resolved to do something to fix my problem.

That something was to try to reshape my chest through exercise and diet. I began to restrict what I ate, both in terms of restricting calories and restricting types of foods. I also started to exercise compulsively. I got a weight bench and would lift weights for hours every night while the rest of my family was asleep.

During this time I started to also develop an obsession with doing things in sets of thirteen, especially exercises. I would lift weights in sets of thirteen and do pushups in sets of thirteen. I felt afraid that something bad would happen if I didn't do things in sets of thirteen.

This continued through high school. When I got to college, my anxiety, secrecy, and shame grew. I began to become obsessed with eating only raw vegetables because I felt that I was "toxic" and that raw vegetables would cleanse me. I read books that affirmed my beliefs rather than going to classes or doing homework. I performed enemas secretly because I thought they would help me with the "cleansing reactions" (i.e. severe fatigue, insomnia, and lightheadedness) that I was experiencing (which were really symptoms of starvation, of course).

The obsessions and compulsions already grew during college. I started to superstitiously avoid stepping on cracks in the sidewalk out of fear that it would actually "break my mother's back". I also started to compulsively turn around in sets of three while taking a shower. I had a vague fear that if I didn't indulge the compulsion, something bad would happen to me or someone I loved.

I dropped out of college suddenly and took a Greyhound bus from Illinois to Los Angeles, California on a whim. Once in California, I eased up on the severity of my eating disorder. Though I still obsessed about food and ate in strange ways, and even though I was still eating too little and not getting adequate nutrition, it wasn't nearly as bad as it had been.

In California I discovered all kinds of alternative lifestyle, health, self-help, and spiritual practices and communities. I learned Transcendental Meditation, which I practiced obsessively many hours every day. I was initiated into a variety of spiritual practices. I practiced hatha yoga daily.

I hoped that these things would help me to feel better. But they didn't. So I sought out more. I worked from home as a computer programmer.

I made lots of money, and that gave me the relative freedom to dedicate hours upon hours every day to meditation, chanting, prayer, yoga, breathwork, and on and on.

I went to all kinds of people in search of help. Therapists, hypnotists, Rebirthing guides, strange palm line therapies, and on and on.

I became paranoid. I was fearful that people were trying to poison me. I was so paranoid that I would booby trap my apartment even while I was there. I was so terrified that someone was hiding and sneaking around in my apartment, tampering with my things. I ordered five-gallon bottles of water for my drinking water, but half the time I'd be so paranoid that someone had poisoned the water that I would dump it down the drain.

I also developed reactions to smells and "chemicals". I felt that I couldn't breathe near many smells. The smells of scented candles, the smells of mattresses, new clothing, old clothing, shampoo, car exhaust, paint, carpets, new cars, old cars, mold, cleaning products...nearly everything. Even neighbors' cooking smells. Trying to protect myself from these smells and chemicals, I tried all kinds of ways to seal off my apartment from the outside, I bought air filter machines, and I avoided some of the places that were the worst offenders (many stores being among the worst).

And I started to develop intense sound sensitivity. The sound of the clock ticking or a distant dog barking would provoke rage. I would feel as though I would explode. I felt horrible and hopeless. I tried to sedate the pain with various practices or herbs or far-out nutritional supplements and quasi-drugs. Nothing worked.

The obsessions worsened. I had learned about numerology and became obsessed with the numerological significance of everything. My name, my address, the subject lines of emails.

When I was planning to move from southern California to Boston, I had an obsession that I needed to keep a California mailing address. So I looked for a mailbox rental that would meet my stringent criteria. It had to have the perfect numerological address, of course. But I also had other criteria. I had developed an obsession with avoiding McDonald's, and I had a rule that the mailbox rental had to be located at least one mile from the nearest McDonald's. I drove far and wife throughout southern California, a task that took many dozens of hours, and I never found anything to meet my criteria.

After I moved to Boston, I met a woman who fell in love with me right away. We got married before she had discovered just how much of a mess I was, and the next year was surely miserable for her. I had so many rigid rules for how things "had to be". I moved from Boston to Frederickton, New Brunswick (Canada). She came with me, but things grew more and more grim. We left Frederickton and moved to Kingston, Ontario. Then to Toronto.

Then I hatched the plan to move into a cargo van and tour the United States. She came with me, and we lasted a few weeks before she had enough. Not only of the cargo van, but of me. She went to live with her mother while recovering from the trauma of having been married to me and she filed for divorce.

The next year or two was a whirlwind of nightmares. I temporarily rented an unfurnished apartment that I left unfurnished except for the plastic tarps that I had taped up everywhere in an attempt to seal off the apartment from all the smells and chemicals that I was afraid of. I would sit on the bare floor and pray and meditate and read books that I hoped would offer some kind of help. But I was restless and in so much pain that I abandoned that apartment and moved back into the cargo van.

I drove around the country in search of *something*. What, I didn't know any longer. Just something that could offer relief. A place. A situation. Anything. I was desperate.

My obsessions had grown to include not only avoiding McDonald's, but also anything that reminded me of McDonald's – a billboard, a McDonald's truck, a piece of trash on the side of the road. Even the colors red and yellow together or the number 9 became associated with McDonald's in my mind. I would panic any time I would see these things. Eventually I would panic if I even thought of them. If the color red would flash in my mind I would have elaborate rituals for trying to "cleanse" myself of it. And I wouldn't allow myself to eat until I felt clean again.

The obsessions expanded beyond McDonald's to include Walmart, Coca-Cola, and sugar. I remember driving around the state of Rhode Island in search of food, but everywhere I went "sugar" was present that would send me into a panic. One day I left a store in a panic because a song over the sound system contained the word "sugar" in the lyrics.

In the winter of 2009-2010, desperate, I went to an "outdoor school" in northern Wisconsin and lived outside in the woods. I was severely malnourished. I couldn't get warm. I was paranoid and obsessing. And I would walk through the woods feeling that maybe I was being guided to find that "something" that would magically cure me.

I didn't find that magical cure. Instead, after the winter, I went back to New England in my cargo van, bought a piece of raw land way out in the woods, and I tried to live out there, sleeping on the ground.

Though this all may sound horrible, I actually felt a small hope during this time. I had not yet discovered the Ease In Method, but I had discovered the precursor, which was transparency and honesty. I realized that my whole life I had been hiding in shame and that I had never really tried simply being fully honest and transparent.

I met a woman during this time, and for the first time in my life I exposed everything. I didn't keep any secrets. I was fully honest about all my challenges, all my fears, all my paranoid thinking. All of it.

This began a relationship that continues to this day. My behavior and choices continued to be challenges in relationship, but full honesty and transparency made a tremendous positive difference. I felt slightly optimistic. And in early June of 2010 we conceived our first child.

It was then that I was bitten by ticks for the first time in my life. I knew nothing about ticks or Lyme disease. But I found out about ticks and Lyme disease pretty quickly. In late June of 2010 I became suddenly, severely ill with a high fever that provoked mild delusions. It lasted only a day or two, but afterward I never felt fully well. Then the bulls eye rashes began. Then the migrating joint swelling and pain. I was 31 years old and could barely get in and out of a car from the swelling and pain.

Those around me knew what it was. They encouraged me to get antibiotic treatment. I refused. I hated myself and felt that I deserved to be punished. I also arrogantly believed I could defeat it through will power.

By the winter of that year, the joint pain and swelling had subsided. I thought I had "won". But then the psychological symptoms began. Everything took on a sense of darkness. It was as if a veil was over my eyes and my mind that filtered out the light and hope in life. If things had been bad before, I had never known things could be so nightmarish as they became.

I grew weaker and weaker. My digestion worsened so that I was having trouble eating. And all my obsessions, compulsions, paranoia, and all the rest of it continued.

Meanwhile, my oldest daughter was born in early Spring 2011. We lived in a small cabin in New Hampshire without running water or electricity. I would hand wash the diapers in near-freezing water that I gathered from the nearby brook. I would count as I would wring out the diapers, trying to wring them an "acceptable" number of times (the acceptable numbers were always changing) without thinking of McDonald's or sugar or any of the other things that were "bad". If I thought of any of the "bad" things, I'd start over with the washing. My hands were often blistered.

Things continued like this until mid-2012. I had become so severely ill that I was unable to eat anything other than half a cup of toasted oats each day. I could barely drink water. I was so weak I would have to try to work up the will to get up off the mattress for sometimes an hour or longer in order to go pee.

I realized that I couldn't continue as I had done. I knew that I wasn't going to find that magical solution or magical place somewhere out there. I had reached a dead end.

Reaching a dead end and not having any hope of escape was one of the greatest blessings of my life.

It was then that I first discovered the early version of the Ease In Method. Of course, I didn't have a name for it. Nor did I understand it well. Nor had I had much practice with it. But it was there in that dead end that I finally found the secret of humility and easing in to direct experience as a process for healing.

I had had glimpses of direct experience in the past. I'd had mentors who pointed it out to me. I'd read books about it. But it had always been just an intellectual exercise or a kind of novelty. I hadn't recognized the power of easing into direct experience for healing. Not until mid-2012 when I was nearly dead.

Then, in desperation, I discovered that rather than trying to fix my problems, I could ease into direct experience and rest in the healing balm of wholeness. The more I explored this, the more alive it became in me.

At first, I was over-complicating it because I was using Emotional Freedom Techniques (tapping) as a method for facilitating this process. But as I allowed it to become simpler and simpler, I realized that I didn't need any complicated process. All that was needed was to ease in to direct experience and simply allow whatever my experience was.

Memories would surface. Images, sensations, feelings, thoughts would float up. And all I needed to do was simply allow it all without grasping or protecting. The more I allowed, the clearer it became that I didn't need to solve my problems. At least not at the level I had been trying to solve them at.

All my problems actually vanished instantly whenever I would rest in direct experience. And the more I would rest in direct experience, the more this actually began to change my life. I began to find that my actions were moved by and informed by wholeness. Rather than trying to fix things, all I had to do was "be here now".

Importantly, I wasn't hiding out in direct experience as a strategy to avoid my problems. I was resting in the wholeness that I discovered in direct experience and allowing that to spill over into my life by moving me and guiding my actions. In practice this has meant the willingness to do things differently, to behave from the clarity of wholeness even when it runs counter to my conditioning. Even when I feel fearful.

Many people imagine that if they could only "wake up" that would instantly solve all their problems. I had mistakenly believed that. But I discovered that I woke up into my life, which included starvation, compulsive behavior, a lot of shame and self-hatred, and a whole lot of other challenges. "Waking up" didn't instantly change those things. What it did was give me conscious access to wholeness and the courage to allow that wholeness to move me into new actions. It gave me access to the willingness and patience to meet the challenges of my life in new ways.

I have had to consistently apply the Ease In Method in my life in order to discover the manifest benefits. But this has unquestionably changed my life for the better. My wife noticed the change right away. And she has told me that had things not changed, she doesn't know how much longer it would have been possible for her to endure the challenges of living with me.

Others around me noticed the changes. And they continued to notice the changes as I further softened and allowed myself to be shaped by this direct connection with wholeness.

Within a few months I was no longer struggling with obsessions or compulsions. Within a few more months I was cured of reactivity to smells and chemicals as well as sound sensitivity. I stopped starving myself and began to love and nourish my body. Everything that I had struggled with for so many years had either completely dissolved or significantly softened.

Fundamentally, I no longer perceived myself as separate or as a victim. This gave me confidence to meet every challenge. And the more challenges I met, the more I started to see challenges as opportunities for healing.

A year later I began to share with others about what I had discovered. It was not easy because I don't particularly like taking on that role. It was and is often uncomfortable. But in mid-2012 when I was at the dead end, I took a vow. Why I did this, I don't know. I think it was coming from gratitude and love deep inside. But I took a vow within myself to share whatever I discover of value with those who struggle and can benefit.

So I have continued to share despite it often feeling awkward and uncomfortable. I have shared through holding meetings, writing books, creating videos, offering trainings, and every means I know of in order to get this message out to people. The message is that healing is possible. Healing is nearer than you think. And it is easier than you think. Not easy in the sense of being comfortable. But easy in the sense that you don't have to struggle or seek for it. It is here. It is found in the humility of your own heart. And it can and will take all your problems and turn them into gifts. It takes patience. It takes courage. It takes willingness. But it is not far off. It is here now. And it gets better and better.

I have had the honor of seeing dozens of people heal from significant suffering in their lives through direct coaching that I've offered over these past seven years. And I've had many more people write to me with their stories of how my books, videos, and trainings have helped them to discover healing.

In the next section, I'll guide you to begin to experience the Ease In Method for yourself.

Part II: The Method

The Shortcut

First, before I write anything else on the subject, I feel it is appropriate to make it clear that there is a shortcut. Everything else that follows is merely an elaboration, an unpacking, of this shortcut. This shortcut is the essence of the Ease In Method. Whenever you are in doubt or if anything that follows confuses you, come back to this shortcut.

The shortcut is not different from what follows. And all that follows only leads back to the shortcut.

One way this is sometimes expressed is that the finger pointing to the moon is not the moon. But the finger pointing to the moon can be useful sometimes in order to discover the moon. Looking directly at the moon is the shortcut. When not yet familiar enough with how to directly look at the moon, following the finger pointing to the moon can be helpful.

The shortcut, which is the essence of the simplicity and directness that the Ease In Method points to is this: this right now is already whole, and your present experience is already of wholeness. If you cease making effort for one moment, this becomes clear. When you catch this glimpse repeatedly, you embody this simple clarity that all is already wholeness and cannot be otherwise. Nothing needs to be done. By continuing to ease in to this wholeness, this wholeness informs your actions and moves you to behave in congruence with wholeness.

It really is that simple. But because it is so simple, most of us can't understand it at first.

For those of us who don't catch the glimpse and trust fully in that instantly right now, there is what follows – many explorations and experiments to catch glimpses and embody the simplicity of the wholeness and directness of what is.

Expectations

Before we get to the practical understanding and application of the Ease In Method, I want to set your expectations correctly. If you have the right expectations, you will experience rapid and consistent benefits with this approach. On the other hand, if you have the wrong expectations, you will likely grow frustrated and abandon the approach, or worse yet, burden yourself with useless and ineffective application of the method.

In other words, proper expectation is essential. Do not skip this section.

In years past, when I was most desperately seeking for solutions to my many, many challenges in life, I read countless books, attended perhaps a hundred or so workshops and retreats, took dozens of trainings, had dozens of initiations into various practices and teachings...and because I failed to have proper understanding and expectations, none of them provided the results I wanted.

The truth is, a superficial application of a process or technique is unlikely to ever work well. The reason is simple: without a proper grounding in the essential discovery or "aha!" of that underlies a process or technique, the mechanics of it won't work. In such cases, the application of the process becomes superstitious and rooted in fear rather than grounded in wholeness – the latter being the essence of true healing.

So hopefully it makes sense to you that if you want true healing, you must first be grounded in the essence of true healing, which is wholeness.

This is the first and most fundamental principle of the Ease In Method – that true healing comes from wholeness and that we must consciously recognize wholeness to experience true, rapid, and sustained healing.

In fact, if you were to do only this one thing persistently, you would discover profound healing at all levels and in all ways. It is that important and that powerful.

But it is important to understand that this takes persistence. And it is also important to understand that you're current understanding of what healing should look and feel like is distorted by years or lifetimes of trauma and wrong understanding. As such, you cannot and must not judge your healing from your conditioned mind.

This can be the most challenging aspect of any true healing, and certainly it is so with the Ease In Method. We are conditioned to be highly reactive and impatient. We want instant relief because we perceive our suffering is intolerable. And although instant relief is available, we miss it because we wrongly interpret that relief as suffering. We are all turned around and upside down and inside out. We are disoriented. When we are willing to commit and have patience, we see clearly.

If you want true healing with the Ease In Method, you must be willing to commit to patient persistence with the Ease In Method. When you make this commitment and follow through with the commitment, the rewards are immense. The rewards are both instantaneous (though impossible for your conscious mind to acknowledge) and progressive. Grounding in wholeness removes the apparent obstacles of time.

This opens you to the paradox that when you are humble and patient and committed, when you are willing to look beyond your conditioned ideas of what healing should be and look like and feel like, you are at once immediately healed and also progressively healed. Both immediate and progressive healing are the result of this correct expectation.

I'm reminded of a story that a meditation teacher told me many years ago. It is a Hindu story, but don't misunderstand this to be a religious teaching. It is a valuable metaphor, and it has stuck with me for nearly 20 years since he first told it to me.

Shiva, who is the supreme being in the Hindu mythology, took form and came to earth. As he walked along a path, he came upon a devotee who upon seeing Shiva fell down on his knees. Shiva bid him to stand. The man said, "Oh, Lord Shiva, I am your devotee, and I dedicate my life to your service. Might I know if I will reach enlightenment, and if so, when?"

To this, Shiva replied, "Yes, you shall, and in just ten lifetimes."

The man was upset to hear this. He said, "Ten lifetimes! But I have dedicated my entire life to worshipping you. Surely this is not fair." After which, the man, in disgust gave up his devotion of Shiva and went in search of some better path in life.

Shiva continued walking on the path and came upon another devotee. As with the first devotee, this man fell down on his knees at the sight of Shiva. Shiva bid the man to stand. And this second devotee said, like the first, "Oh, Lord Shiva, I am your devotee, and I dedicate my life to your service. Might I know if I will reach enlightenment, and if so, when?"

To this, Shiva replied, "Yes, you shall, and it will take one hundred lifetimes."

The second devotee was overjoyed. He thanked Shiva profusely, "Oh, Lord Shiva, I am so grateful to hear this good news."

When I first heard this story, I didn't like it at all. I felt angry that anyone would suggest that it should be necessary to have such patience as well as such gratitude when it seemed so *unfair* that the gratification shouldn't be immediate.

But twenty years later – and after having abandoned many paths out of impatience - I understand and appreciate this story in a new way. Commitment, persistence, and patience are virtues that yield both long term benefits as well as *immediate* benefits.

This is impossible to understand as long as we cling to impatience, anger, and arrogance. It takes true humility to admit that our ideas and beliefs aren't the truth or necessarily even what is best.

In fact, what true humility reveals – and what the Ease In Method will show you if you allow it – is that what is best is what is. What is here now, this present experience, including all our present reactivity, sensations, impulses, and so on are absolutely perfect and it opens us to both instantaneous healing as well as progressive healing.

The real key is to be willing to allow it all and *ease in* to the underlying unified field of wholeness that holds it all, allows it all, and is the essential nature of all that is. (In other words, we ease in to the recognition that we are already indistinguishable from wholeness in direct experience. We don't falsely claim that we are wholeness. Rather, we recognize that wholeness is all that is, and anything appearing otherwise is merely a conceptual overlay.) When we do this, we discover immediately the perfection of this moment as it is and the perfection of ourselves as we are right now. And at the same time, we discover the humility to admit that we (in appearance and in concept) are simultaneously growing and evolving and maturing.

When we are humble enough, we discover that our lives aren't strictly for us alone. Our lives are in service to that underlying unified wholeness that desires to expand creation and manifest its attributes such as love, connection, freedom, and peace. Please don't take this on as a belief. I am merely sharing what my experience of this is and what I believe you will discover for yourself when you ease in to your true nature as indistinguishable from wholeness.

Take my own life as an example. Twenty years ago, when I felt so angry about the story of Shiva and the devotees, I was impatient because I saw my life as only for me. I viewed my experiences as being for me alone, and anything I perceived as unpleasant, frustrating, painful, or discouraging seemed like it was wrong.

And yet through those difficult experiences, I have been tempered. I have matured. I have softened. And my life has come to be in service to something much greater. In the past seven years I have had the great honor to serve hundreds of people and help many of them to discover greater peace and freedom in their lives.

My life is not for me alone. My life is for life itself. My life is in service of the whole in all its forms.

This is a joy that is far greater than the mere relief of unwanted symptoms. To serve others and to discover ever greater humility is the greatest joy I have ever known. And what makes it even better is that I am far from perfect, so I know that there is so much more to grow and discover and give. So much more wisdom to receive and share. So much more love to wake up to and spread as a healing balm.

Not that I don't have moments of forgetfulness or frustration or impatience. I do. But my life experience shows me over and over that what is truer than any of my shortsighted reactivity is a greater wholeness that is love and that I am always one with. Like a drop of water is never separate from the ocean.

This is the right expectation. Expect that patience and commitment will yield instantaneous recognition as well as progressive maturity and softening. Any time you indulge impatience, you will find that, as in the experiment that I'll share with you in the next section, you'll experience yourself as pushed to the surface. Whereas, any time you ease in, you'll find that your experience of yourself softens and becomes fluid.

The Oobleck Experiment

When I was a kid, I remember experiencing wonder in many instances. One simple experiment from my childhood that I want to encourage you to do involves something called Oobleck, named after the imaginary substance from a Dr. Seuss book.

Please don't skip this experiment. Don't just refer to your memory of having played with Oobleck as a child or perhaps as a parent or merely witnessing the wonder of another playing with it. There is no substitute for the actual experience of something.

Here's what you'll need: two parts starch (cornstarch or potato starch both work), one part water, and one bowl large enough to hold the mixture. One cup starch to half a cup of water is a good amount in most cases.

Mix the starch and the water together (very slowly) in the bowl.

You now have Oobleck. Now it is time to play and experience wonder.

Start cautiously if you prefer by simply touching your hand to the Oobleck. Then let the moment move you. Let yourself press it, squeeze it, etc. (Though you may prefer not to get it in your hair, on your clothes, or on your furniture. You are allowed to retain some of your adult conservatism and "common sense".)

Do this now before you read more. Seriously. Don't read on until you do it.

I'm assuming you aren't cheating (yourself) and that you've now experimented with the Oobleck.

What you've almost certainly discovered in your own experience is that if you move your finger or hand quickly or use a lot of force, the Oobleck firms up and provides resistance. But if you move very slowly, the Oobleck behaves like a liquid.

Again, there is no substitute for the actual experience. So please be sure to do this experiment. This will give you an experience in your bodymind that will allow you to more easily translate this experience to other dimensions of being.

Dimensions of Being and Direct Experience

Chances are, you've heard of the so-called five senses: sight, smell, taste, touch, and hearing. But most of us have not taken the time to explore these senses as well as our other dimensions of being in direct experience. Instead, we are accustomed to only filtering these experiences through a conceptual overlay.

The implication of filtering our experiences through a conceptual overlay is that we believe that our conditioning is truth and we wrongly imagine ourselves to be cut off from wholeness. As a result, we don't even recognize wholeness. We think of wholeness as being something other than what is already the case. And because of this we suffer and we overlook true healing.

What I'd like to invite you to discover in your own direct experience is the present reality of wholeness. And I'll guide you in this section to explore this for yourself.

For some of this exploration, it will likely be easiest for you to discover what I am guiding you to if you have your eyes closed. For the next few paragraphs, I'll give you some guidance and then ask you to close your eyes and explore what I've just guided you in.

To begin with, let's explore sound and hearing. In subsequent sections we'll explore other dimensions, but sound is often easiest to explore. (With that said, if sound and hearing are inaccessible for you, you can adapt this same exploration to other senses. We'll look at touch/sensation and sight/seeing in later sections.) In just a moment, I'll ask you to close your eyes and notice whatever you notice in the field of sound and hearing. For the next minute or two, simply notice. Close your eyes and do this now. When you are done, open your eyes and continue reading.

You may have noticed many things. Among the things you may have noticed is that (if you are like the rest of us) you automatically label and have stories about what you are aware of in the field of sound and hearing.

What I mean when I say "label and have stories" may not be immediately clear, so let me elaborate briefly. Right now, as I type this, I am standing in a room with my children and wife and our dog. I am aware of sounds and hearing, and I am aware of labels and stories such as "my daughter's voice", "coming from over there", "I am over here", "laughter", "interrupting", "alliteration", "pleasing", "singing", "too much", "overwhelming", "difficult to concentrate".

Now, let's try exploring sound a second time. As before, do this with eyes closed. And with awareness of labels and stories, just notice the labels and stories. Do this now for a minute or two, then open your eyes and continue reading.

If you are observant, you'll notice that these labels and stories are all conditioned and conceptual. They all are based on the assumptions that time, space, and separation are fundamentally real and that you are a separate object *here* while the sounds are other separate objects *out there.*

Now, let's begin to observe sound and hearing non-conceptually. This time, with eyes closed, notice that you are simply aware of sound and hearing even without the labels and stories. Importantly, I am not suggesting that you should make any effort to get rid of labels or stories. The labels and stories simply happen, and that is okay. Rather, somewhat like slowly sinking your finger into Oobleck and letting it rest there, let yourself ease into the direct experience of hearing and sound. Then just rest in this direct experience without reacting or grasping at any label or story. Let the labels and stories happen as they do, but notice that you can be at rest momentarily and just be aware of the direct experience of sound and hearing. Please close your eyes and observe in this way for a minute or two. When you are done, open your eyes and continue reading.

Hopefully this gives you a gentle sense of easing into the direct experience that is impermanent and non-objective. It is simply happening here and now. It is not something you can grasp or understand. But it is true and real and immediately recognizable. You don't have to make any effort to recognize this. It is just obvious. Sound and hearing happening.

Next, let's explore this a little more in depth. This time, with eyes closed and resting in the direct experience, I'd like you to explore if you can find a location for the sound or hearing that is non-conceptual. Of course, your nervous system will give you information that you will interpret – out of conditioned habit – as having location. Sounds *seem* to be out there or over there. But if you simply ease in to the direct experience and rest here for a moment, notice if there is any non-conceptual proof of location. Or is location and separation – here and there – object and subject – just a conceptual overlay that you've assumed to be true? Please close your eyes and explore this for a minute or two. When you are done, open your eyes and continue reading.

If you truly rest in direct experience for a moment – not turning to a concept, thought, or idea for an answer – this might be a strange experience. It might be slightly unsettling not to be able to find a location for yourself or a sound. It might be disorienting. If so, that is okay. This is part of a re-orientation process. You are shifting from identifying as a concept to recognizing that in direct experience there is only this as it is, and it is not graspable or knowable. It simply is. You simply are.

Let's now explore the limits or boundaries of hearing and sound. This time, again with eyes closed, I'd like you to explore in your direct experience to see if you can find a boundary to this field of hearing/sound. Can you find a non-conceptual boundary to hearing or sound? Is there a non-conceptual beginning or end to the field of hearing? Is there a non-conceptual beginning or end to sound? Close your eyes and observe for a minute or two. When you are done, open your eyes and continue reading.

For most of us, it is not difficult to discover in direct experience that there is no beginning or end – no boundary – to hearing itself. Hearing is clearly simply happening, and it has no edges.

Sometimes people get hung up on sound itself, though. Sometimes people cling to the idea that a sound is a discrete thing that has a beginning and an end. And the reason for this is that *conceptually* it does have a beginning and an end. To speak of "a sound" implies that it is an object, and all objects have beginnings and ends both in time and space. You can perform a simple experiment: clap your hands and listen to "the sound".

The sound of a clap has a beginning and an end in time...conceptually. There is the moment before the beginning of the sound. Then the sound. Then no sound. And so we assume that there is such a thing as a sound and that it must have a beginning and an end.

But in this exploration, we are looking to explore in direct experience – *not* conceptually. Because most people have such a strong habit of filtering everything through concept, they immediately leap to concept and don't recognize that the direct experience reveals that there is no discrete thing called a sound that we can actually find.

So try it a few times. Close your eyes, and clap your hands, leaving a few seconds between each clap. Observe to see if you can find the sound itself as a thing. And observe to see if you can find where it comes from and goes to. Please do that now and then open your eyes and continue reading.

This experiment defies our common way of understanding things. You might even grow frustrated and believe this is silly or "insane". But that is only because we are in the habit of filtering our experience through concept, which seeks to objectify our experience. We mistake the conceptual filter for primary reality and because our actual direct experience doesn't conform to the conceptual filter, we grow impatient and frustrated.

However, what I am pointing you to discover for yourself is that what is truer is that direct experience is primary. The conceptual filter is merely that: a conceptual filter.

Just as Newtonian physics is a useful model that allows us to predict how things will move but it is not the whole truth and there are many examples of things that don't conform to Newtonian models, so too is the conceptual and conditioned filter a useful tool that allows us to predict and react in (sometimes) useful and functional ways, it is not the whole truth or the primary reality. It is merely a model and filter. When we understand it correctly, we can make use of it to our benefit.

When we misunderstand it, we suffer and wrongly perceive ourselves as separate and victims.

Let's now do one more exploration together with sound and hearing. This time with eyes open. Up to now we've had eyes closed to make it easier to focus on hearing and sound. But I don't want to mislead you into believing that this is only available to us with eyes closed. So now, keeping your eyes open, notice how in direct experience sound and hearing continues to have no location, no boundary, no labels, no stories. It is simply happening as a unified experience. There is flow. Sound is silence and silence is sound. There is no separation between sound and hearing and hearer.

Before we move on, I want to remind you again that the purpose of this investigation is to help you to ease in to direct experience and discover ever-present wholeness. Don't make the mistake of thinking that it is necessary to cease to perceive sound as having location, direction, and other qualities that you are conditioned to perceive. That is all perfectly fine and appropriate for normal functioning. What we are doing here is simply exploring to discover that beyond the conditioned perception there is this unified field of wholeness that is effortlessly available to us. This is simply an exploration that is a means to an end. Remember that training wheels are not the same as riding a bicycle. So too, in kind of inquiry is merely a means, no the thing itself.

Sensation in Direct Experience

The reason we started our exploration of direct experience with sound was because typically people are less reactive to sound than they are to seeing or sensation. But our aim with this investigation is to discover the possibility of easing into non-reactivity and the direct experience of wholeness without relying on the conceptual filter. And because of that, we're going to explore other dimensions of being, including sensation.

For most of us, most of the time, we are filtering our sensations through the conceptual filter so automatically and quickly that we don't even know that we're doing it.

The best thing we can do here is just begin to explore. So in just a moment I'll ask you to close your eyes again. When you do, I'd like you to take a minute or two to just notice sensation in direct experience, without the conceptual filter. As before, I'm not asking you to get rid of concepts or thoughts. I'm just inviting you to explore what is more direct and immediate in regard to sensation. Let's do that now. Close your eyes and explore this for a moment. When you're done, open your eyes and read on.

You may have noticed any number of things. After coaching hundreds of people in this exploration, what most have reported to me initially is that they notice the labels and stories about the sensations. They report that they noticed tings like "the feeling of sitting in a chair" or "the feeling of my hand resting on my lap" or "the sensation of itching on my nose".

If that's what you noticed, that's not bad or wrong. But it is conceptual. What I'm inviting you to discover is what is non-conceptual. There is the raw sensation that you may interpret through the conceptual filter as being, for example, the sensation of sitting in a chair. But perhaps you can notice that the raw sensation is pure sensation and does not actually have that meaning that the label or story suggests. You could imagine for a moment what it might be like to be an infant with no experience of knowledge of "chair" or "me" or "sitting". In such a case, you would not have the story or label to apply as a filter. You'd only have the raw experience of the sensation.

The sensation is real and happens independent of the conceptual filter. You can discover and recognize this for yourself.

Whether you already noticed this or not, let's explore once again. Close your eyes for a minute or two and simply tune into the raw sensation that you notice without latching on to any concept or idea. Do that now, and when you're done, open your eyes and continue reading.

As with when exploring sound and hearing, you might find that initially this can feel slightly disorienting. You might be so in the habit of filtering everything conceptually that you have, like many of us, fallen into the habit of mistaking the conceptual for primary. Whereas, in fact, the raw sensation is prior to and more primary. Without the raw sensation the conceptual overlay would have no sense of substance. It wouldn't seem to refer to anything real. It would be pure abstraction. The direct experience of the raw sensation is what gives substance to the experience.

So if you feel disoriented or notice that the habit of turning to concept as the primary reality is still strong, don't worry. Continue to explore in this way and it becomes clearer and easier to recognize what is primary.

This is not to suggest that the conceptual overlay is bad or wrong or inherently harmful. It is actually quite useful to be able to understand and use concepts as long as they align well with reality. But if you've ever had the experience of thinking there was one step more or less than there really was when going down a staircase, you know the problems that can arise from a mismatch between the conceptual overlay and reality. So while conceptual filters applied to sensation can be useful when they allow us to function rapidly in ways that are efficient and non-harmful, that is great. But when there I a mismatch, things can go badly.

Our exploration here is designed to give you greater flexibility so that you can readily have access to the direct experience and not rely solely on the conceptual filter.

Here's a practical example of how this can be useful. People who have had limbs amputated often struggle with a phenomenon known as phantom limb pain. That means they experience pain that their nervous systems suggest to them is located in the amputated limb. In other words, a person with no right leg can believe that they are experiencing pain – sometimes excruciating pain – in their right foot. They can look down and see that they have no right foot, but their brain keeps telling them that they are experiencing pain in the right foot that they don't have.

The conventional understanding of pain that most people have is actually a misunderstanding. Pain is an interpretation that the nervous system makes. Pain is a product of the nervous system. And when we understand this, we can more easily understand how a person can experience pain that seems to be in their foot that they don't have.

Not only that, but it hints at a possible solution. And, in fact, this is a real, practical solution to phantom limb pain. We can't address pain in a foot that doesn't exist. But we can alter the conditioning in the nervous system. And we can do this through inquiry. And, by the way, this applies not only to phantom limb pain. This applies to all sensation. Through inquiry we can discover directly that pain is a product of the nervous system mediated by attention stuck on a conceptual filter.

Before we try to get ahead of ourselves and cure ourselves of all pain, let's reign it in and just return to a simple inquiry. The reason I mentioned everything in the past few paragraphs was simply to demonstrate that this is not merely abstract theory. This has practical application. When there is a mismatch between the model and the reality we can benefit by having access to direct experience rather than filtering everything through old, conditioned, (often painful) concepts.

In the spirit of the phantom limb discussion, let's next explore the location of sensation. With eyes closed, I'd like you to see if you can find a non-conceptual location for sensation. Of course, you'll likely have conceptual responses that provide a location for sensation such as tension in your back or heaviness in your stomach or tickling in your toes. But without turning to a concept, can you find proof of a location for sensation? Close your eyes and explore this for a minute or two. When you're done, open your eyes and continue reading.

By now it is probably getting clearer that when attention is stuck on the conceptual filter, it produces a self-reinforcing loop in which the experience is imagined to be proof of the concept. For example, if you had a sensation that you believed was an itch on your right big toe and I asked you how you know that the sensation means what you think it means, the only reason you could give would be that "I feel it and it feels like it is in my right big toe and it feels like an itch."

That's functional *if* scratching the right big toe relieves the sensation. But what if it doesn't relieve the sensation? When if you keep scratching until your right big toe is bleeding and it gets infected and that still doesn't relieve the sensation? Then it is clearly not functional. And unfortunately, that is the kind of scenario that we find ourselves in far too often – with sensation as well as, as we'll see soon enough, emotion and other dimensions of being.

If scratching the itch doesn't provide immediate and lasting relief and it instead results in pain, discomfort, restriction, fear, trauma, etc., we will benefit from cultivating greater flexibility in our ability to shift to direct experience and find deeper relief. If the conceptual filter is simply wrong or ineffective or inefficient, continuing to depend on it is only going to result in harm.

Without concept, there is no location for sensation. There is merely the raw sensation.

Next, let's explore the boundaries of sensation. This is very closely related to location. But often, even after we discover in direct experience that sensation doesn't have a location, we can still wrongly imagine that sensation has boundaries. So here's what you can do next. Close your eyes and notice if you can find a boundary – a beginning or end – to a sensation. See if you can find a sensation that is distinct from another supposed sensation. Conceptually, of course, you may believe that there is a sensation that is called pain and then another sensation elsewhere that is called ease. But see if you can find the actual boundary to any supposed sensation in direct experience. Do that for a minute or two now. When you're done, open your eyes and continue reading.

I just want to take a moment to remind you of the importance of truly exploring these things. Just conceptually coming to a conclusion about these things is not a substitute for truly exploring. So please be sure that you are truly doing these explorations.

When you explore in this direct, non-conceptual way, it becomes clear that there is no directly-findable boundary. There is only conceptual boundary. But in direct experience there is simply sensation or sensing, and there is no distinct sensation that is separate from another sensation – neither in space nor in time. There is just direct sensing happening.

Again, this doesn't jibe with our conceptual overlay. And it doesn't need to. So please don't make the mistake of trying to alter your conceptual filter to do away with conceptual distinctions and separation. That is the function of concept. And it can be quite functional. Being able to locate a sensation in the body conceptually is often useful. It allows you to scratch an itch, brush away a mosquito, and other functional things.

But it is only a small part of the total reality that we all have an intimate relationship with. And when we overlook the totality in favor of a small fraction of reality – particularly when we forget that the totality exists apart from the conceptual filter – we can suffer needlessly. When we open to and ease in to the direct experience, we can discover flexibility and freedom that allows us to begin to live and move and act in accordance with our deeper, most authentic desires. Rather than being restricted to old, limiting, reactive patterns, we gain access to something far greater.

Emotions and Direct Experience

Now that we've explored sound and sensation, let's next look at emotion.

Experts who study emotion argue about how many emotions there are. For our purposes here, it doesn't matter. We can simply notice that in our own experience we seem to have different emotions, and we could probably agree that at the very least we have the emotions of fear and joy. We could use different words. Instead of joy we could call it love or happiness. Or we could say that we have positive and negative emotions – emotions that are attractive and emotions that are aversive.

Of course, we know we have emotions because of feeling or sensation, so in the truest sense, we could argue that there is no separate emotional dimension. And, of course, it is ultimately true (as we'll explore together later) that there is no findable distinction outside of concept between any of these dimensions of being. So don't get hung up on details here. We're just exploring in a playful, curious way. There's no right or wrong.

In this playful spirit, I'd like you to close your eyes and notice what emotions you notice. And rather than trying to label the emotion, just explore in an open way. See if you can simply tune into the subtler nature of emotion in your direct experience. This should be somewhat easy and familiar to you now that you've been exploring in direct experience. Close your eyes and do that now, and when you're done please open your eyes and read on.

It is sometimes said that emotion is e-motion, or energy in motion. Do you notice that in your experience? Again, there is no right or wrong answer. There is only whatever you actually notice. However, you may find that underneath whatever other ideas you may have, there is simply a sense of either attraction or aversion. Energy or an impulse toward or away from the present experience.

If you notice this fundamental energy in motion, you may also inquire directly in your own, non-conceptual experience with curiosity as to what this motion or direction or orientation *means*. What I intend by this is that normally we believe our conceptual filters about the meaning of the emotions. We typically believe that we know the name of the emotion – fear, joy, hatred, happiness, sadness, etc. – and what that means. We think that fear, for example, means something bad while joy means something good.

But what I'd like to explore together now is what we notice about the meaning of emotion or energetic orientation in direct experience. With eyes closed, explore to see if you can find a non-conceptual meaning to emotion. When you are done, open your eyes and read on.

In direct experience, I find no inherent meaning in emotion. I only find conditioned reactivity. When emotion has an attractive orientation, my conditioning is to move toward something that I associate with the emotion. When the emotion has an aversive orientation, my conditioning is to move away from something that I associate with the emotion. But in direct experience, those meanings are clearly based only on conditioning – not based on inherent meaning that I can find non-conceptually.

Of course, like so much of our conditioning, this can be quite useful. It is typically quite useful to react to an attack by fighting or fleeing. That conditioning has helped countless generations to survive, which has allowed us to be here now. So there is no need to get rid of most of this conditioning.

But when we believe that the label and meaning that is in our conditioning as the one and only truth, when we *only* seem to have access to our conditioned reactivity, we can suffer if the conditioning is not a good match for reality. Here's an example. Many people experience what is called "social anxiety". They desire to connect with others, but because they believe that what they are experiencing is fear and that fear means they should avoid whatever they perceive to be the object of the fear, they avoid social situations. As a result, the don't have opportunities to connect with others.

When we try to overcome our conditioned reactions, we typically try to force ourselves to do what we don't want to do. Given enough repetition, this approach does sometimes work. But far more often, it fails to work. And in many cases it only results in more traumatization.

A gentler approach is far more effective and much more nurturing. Through the kind of direct inquiry that we're exploring together in this book, we can discover, as you may have discovered by now, that the conditioning is merely conditioning. It is not the truth. It is conditioning. And when we are willing to ease in to the direct experience, we get to discover the flexibility to act from clarity and from our most authentic desires.

This is not always easy at first because of the habit of indulging our reactivity. We are often so reactive that we don't even recognize that there is space to pause, ease in, and live and move from clarity and with gentleness for ourselves. But as we continue to commit to easing in to our direct experience, this becomes easier and easier.

Check it out again now. This time with eyes open. Whatever your orientation is to whatever is happening – whether attractive or aversive – can you find any non-conceptual proof that that orientation is the absolute truth? Or is it merely that the orientation is conditioned?

Sometimes this requires repeated and dedicated direct inquiry to gain confidence that really, truly, what you think your emotions mean isn't the truth about what they mean. They don't mean anything. They are merely conditioned reactivity. Sometimes useful. Often not useful.

If your conditioned reactivity, preferences, habits, etc. are functional and in line with your deepest desires – if your life is working out consistently in ways that affirm wholeness, happiness, inner ease, and peace – then great. In that case, there is no need to do anything differently...at least not presently. But if and when your reactivity generates suffering for you and others, you will find benefit in discovering in that moment that infinitely many alternative possibilities exist for you. All that is needed is to ease in to direct experience and then begin to allow yourself to be moved by your deeper, more authentic desires- the desires for peace, connection, freedom, joy, aliveness, and so on.

Importantly, I am not in any way advocating for the suppression or shame of any emotion. In particular, the so-called negative emotions that we typically label as anger, fear, and sadness are ones that we are so strongly conditioned to suppress or shame that it is too easy for us to mistakenly believe that the purpose of any inquiry or method such as the Ease In Method should be to get rid of the emotions.

Please understand that is not the point of the Ease In Method. The point is not to get rid of or suppress or reject or deny or any other variant on that theme. Rather, the point I to ease in to the unconditioned, raw essence. The raw energy or power. At this point in the process, that is all we are doing. Soon, we will discover how to allow the raw, unconditioned energy to then move us in ways that are in alignment with our true desires. Rather than pitting our true desires against the raw emotions, we are tapping into the essence of the raw emotions and letting that be in alignment with our true desires. Our true desires for peace aren't opposed to the emotion that we label as anger, for example. But we can't get that until we ease in to the raw essence, the pure energy.

Seeing in Direct Experience

For those of us who are sighted, we commonly rely on seeing quite extensively. And because we are so reliant on it, we rarely inquire into seeing in direct experience. Instead, we commonly believe that we are seeing objects. In other words, we filter raw seeing through a conceptual overlay and believe that the conceptual overlay is the primary reality.

Like all other dimensions of being, using a conceptual filter for seeing is not bad. It is not inherently harmful. So we are not seeking here to get rid of the conceptual filter or to only ever see without the conceptual filter. Seeing "a dog" or "a cup" or "a person" is not necessarily a problem or something you should try to get rid of.

However, when you don't know how to see non-conceptually or even recognize that you have the capacity and that direct, non-conceptual seeing is primary, you can suffer needlessly. Discovering non-conceptual seeing offers you greater flexibility and adaptability.

As with other dimensions that we've already explored, let's now explore seeing in a variety of ways to gain clarity on the actual nature of seeing and restore our flexibility and adaptability.

To start, let's explore space in the visual field. We typically assume that we exist in space – that we are here and other things are over there, at a distance in space from us. But what do we find in direct experience of simply seeing? For the next minute or two, look outward and see if you can find distance between you and anything else in direct experience. That is, can you find distance except for a concept? When you are done exploring this, continue reading.

In direct experience what you likely have discovered is that there is no evidence of distance. There is only this present seeing happening. Distance is a conceptual overlay. We each learned, most of us very early on, how to interpret what we see through a conceptual filter that tells us how far or near things are to our (imagined) vantage point that we come to understand as here. In this way, here becomes a location that is separate from there. Here is defined by what is not there and there is what is not here.

Now let's explore to see if we can find the actual boundaries of here. As you look outward for a minute or two, explore to see if you can find the boundary of here versus there. Where does here begin and end? What defines here? Is there any non-conceptual boundary? When you are done, continue reading.

What you may discover is that here has no non-conceptual boundary. And, in fact, there is no there to be found separate from here. There is only this present seeing, which has no non-conceptual boundaries.

Next, let's explore objects in direct experience. Objects can be quite functional. It is useful to understand my body as an object and a cup as an object and to be able to pick up the cup object with my body object. So there is no need to perceive all that is as some sort of amorphous goo. That would be non-functional and silly. In fact, in some spiritual traditions, there are precautions that before one attains "higher levels of enlightenment" it is essential to have support systems if the person is to continue to live as a human on account of that person may cease to be very functional in the normal sense.

However, as with all the things we are exploring, when we believe that objects have primary existence, we miss out on flexibility that can allow us to tune into greater ease and freedom. So here we are going to explore in direct experience whether we can find objects other than in concept to let us discover greater ease. Don't make the mistake of turning this into some sort of novelty or intellectual puzzle. That's not the point, and at that level it won't do you any good. But if you let this further release your conditioned habit of getting stuck in a conceptual overlay, you'll find this gives you more freedom in your experience.

For a minute, look at your hand. And as you do, explore to see if you can find the edge or boundary of the hand non-conceptually. This is a funny exploration that can lead to some mind-bending experiences. But just lightly see if you can actually find a non-conceptual boundary for the hand. Do that now and when you're done, continue reading.

Of course, your mind is likely to insist that there is a boundary. Mine does too. So you're in good company (if you consider me good company, that is). But if we tell the truth, that is only a concept. In direct experience, there is only this present seeing. Conceptually we can say that the skin is the boundary. We could say that the contrast of what seems to be solid with what seems to be space is a boundary. We could make lots of conceptual arguments. But non-conceptually, there is only this present seeing.

Again, this is not intended to be a parlor trick or just some intellectual novelty. And there is no benefit to be had in insisting that you have no hand and that hands don't exist. Because while that may be true in some sense, that knowledge in and of itself doesn't do us any real good. So the point here is simply to notice how we have been entranced by the conceptual overlay and yet our direct experience demonstrates that the primary reality is simply of this present seeing – not of objects.

Objects are conceptual. Seeing itself is non-conceptual. Seeing is primary. Objects are a conceptual overlay propped up by and reinforced by the primary reality that we experience as seeing. Yet the seeing itself has no proof of objects.

If your mind is still insisting that you have a hand and that the hand has a boundary, that is okay. That's the sign that you are still functional. That's probably a good thing. So don't worry about it. We're no trying to get rid of anything here...except the unnecessary burden of believing that your conditioned beliefs are the primary reality.

Let's look at the hand again and do another brief experiment with the hand. Look at your hand for a few seconds, then turn the hand. Notice how you can know that you are looking at a hand or that it is the same hand once it is turned without turning to a concept. Do that now, then continue reading.

Philosophically, we get around this by arguing that there is an archetype for a hand that let's us know that what we're looking at is a hand and that my hand and your hand are both hands and that regardless of how the hand is positioned relative to the viewer we can still know it is a hand. That is fine and perhaps interesting as a philosophical puzzle. But in direct experience, we can tell a closer, more intimate truth, which is that without conceptual filtering there is just this present seeing.

In direct experience, the "hand" that we see isn't there. And when we turn the "hand", what now appears is not the same. It is different. The "hand" that was there a moment ago is gone, replaced by this new appearance. Only through concept do we know it is a hand or the same hand. Again, this is functional and not inherently a problem. But we are exploring to gain flexibility.

Now, let's do one more simple experiment. Just look outward and notice for a moment or two that all this present seeing is whole and unified. It is happening without any separation except in concept. Apart from conceptual filters that tell you that there is here and there, this and that, etc., there is only this unified, unbounded present seeing. Let yourself be open to this direct perception for a minute. Then continue to the next section.

Thoughts and Thinking in Direct Experience

By now, it should be getting clear that everything that occurs for you is occurring in direct experience. That is to say, there is nothing that is conceptual as its primary reality. We've explored sound, sensation, emotion, and seeing in direct experience.

Lest you believe that thinking and the conceptual overlay is somehow separate and not also happening as a unified whole in direct experience, let's also briefly explore thinking.

Normally, we give our attention to the superficial level of thinking, entranced by the illusion of thought as the primary reality of thinking. We believe that thoughts are things, and we give a lot of energy to trying to figure out, understand, and manage thoughts. When we do that, we miss out on a deeper level of thinking that reveals its nature to be whole and unbounded and flowing.

Let's now explore thinking in direct experience. The first experiment that I can think of (see what I just did there?) is a simple one: for the next minute or two, observe your thinking and notice if you can find the start or end of a thought. In other words, see if you can find the actual boundaries of a thought. Do that now, either with eyes open or closed (whichever is easier for you) and then continue reading when you're done.

After you've done this experiment, you probably have discovered that you cannot find an actual beginning or end of a thought. Like all the other explorations we've done, the only boundary that we can find is a conceptual boundary. This is quite a funny thing because the concept itself that we have to latch on to in order to define a boundary is, itself, another thought which has no boundary except in another concept.

When we ease in to the direct experience and just notice what is happening, we start to discover that even thoughts are happening as a unified, unbounded, whole. The appearance of thoughts as things is actually something we generate by means of how we focus our attention. When we focus our attention in a particular way, thoughts seem to be things. But as soon as we ease in to direct experience, the thoughts that we thought were things again reveal themselves to be undifferentiated.

Next, let's see if we can become familiar with how we do this objectification or conceptualization. For a minute or two, observe your thinking and each time you notice "a thought", see if you can carefully observe how this thought seems to come into existence and how it seems to disappear from existence. In other words, where does it come from and where does it go and what is the process by which that happens? Do that now and when you are done continue reading.

When you observe carefully, you might notice that each "thought" seems to arise from undifferentiated wholeness and returns to that same undifferentiated wholeness. And perhaps you have also noticed that this comes about through how you direct your attention. When you direct your attention "upward" (don't get hung up on the word) or in a contracted way, a thought seems to take shape. Then the thought falls back into undifferentiated wholeness.

When our attention is chronically tense, uptight, or contracted or fixated in a particular way, we perceive only thought objects while overlooking the undifferentiated wholeness that is the essence of all that is appearing.

Yet through easing in, we tune into the undifferentiated wholeness that underlies everything. This is not difficult. It is not complicated. It is profoundly easy, in fact. It merely requires noticing and not following the compulsion to fixate on objects. In other words, it is deeply restful.

The Unified Nature of All Dimensions

All dimensions of being are one. That includes sound, taste, smell, touch, sensation, sight, emotion, feeling, thought, memory, imagination, and so on.

But please don't take my word for it. Explore this for yourself. For a minute or two, observe in direct experience and see if you can find any boundary between any dimension of your experience. Can you find a non-conceptual boundary between thought and sensation? Between memory and imagination? Between seeing and hearing? Between energy and sound? Do this now and then continue reading when you are ready.

Now that you have explored these seemingly distinct dimensions in direct experience and discovered their unified nature, you have the secret that allows you to begin to make use of the Ease In Method. You know within your own direct experience that you have access to this wholeness at all times. There is nothing outside the wholeness that is found in direct experience.

In some sense, this recognition, this singular glimpse, is all that is needed to provide you with the freedom, ease, and connection that you most desire. That is because in this instant of recognition, you can discover that this wholeness is all that is and that it is always the case. But in practice, we usually benefit from additional support beyond this singular glimpse. In the remainder of the book we'll explore additional support and how you can make use of this recognition in practical ways.

The Somatic Aspect of the Ease In Method

In my experience and from my perspective, it is most useful to discover and make use of what I call the somatic aspect of the Ease In Method.

The term somatic, as I use it, refers to the felt sense of having existence in space. Now, of course, we've already inquired to discover that in direct experience we don't find that we are in space. We don't find a thing at all. But that doesn't negate that we simultaneously have this somatic experience.

One of the major problems (as I see it) of much of so-called non-dual inquiry is that is often becomes a negation of our experience rather than an easing into the wholeness that allows for all of it without a problem. We can take inquiry too far into a purely abstract or intellectual exercise that becomes useless. Or worse yet, it can become harmful.

You can inquire discover that what you think of as water flowing from a faucet is revealed to not exist at all as water or a faucet in direct experience. And yet if you place your hand (despite there being no hand in direct experience) under the water, it gets wet.

Or, to better illustrate how an over-intellectualization of direct inquiry can become actually harmful, you can gaze upon a flame and discover that in direct experience there is no fire. And yet if you place your hand in the flame, you will get burned.

So rather than trying to negate or deny the reality of anything, I believe that the real value of inquiry comes from discovering flexibility and inclusivity. All these seemingly conflicting things co-exist as truths at different perspectives. But the larger perspective found in direct experience is inclusive of all without having to negate any of it.

I find that discovering the somatic aspect to the Ease In Method – a inwardly felt sense that we can become familiar with – allows us a direct, immediate, and highly accessible (and effective) means to ease in to direct experience.

Somatics is a field of exploration of its own, and it is far too great to cover in depth in this book. I'll share with you later in the book how to make more extensive use of somatics as an adjunct to the Ease In Method. However, in this section, I want to introduce you to a simple, three-point process that I developed a number of years ago that I call Somatic Self-Inquiry. This simple process works very well as a means to readily make use of the Ease In Method and to avoid one of the common errors that people make with inquiry of this sort by merely intellectualizing it.

As I suggested earlier, and as you may have noticed for yourself, when we tune into the conceptual filter, we do so through a subtle effort. At the somatic level, we can experience this as a kind of tension. Take a moment now to close your eyes and notice if you feel any inner tension.

For most of us, our habit is to try to fix tension with more tension. We try to force things to let go. Or we try to push it away or ignore it through more tension.

With this process of Somatic Self-Inquiry, which I am presenting to you here in a very concise way, we soften and allow ourselves to ease in without force. This lets the knots of tension unravel on their own.

What I've found – and you can test this for yourself – is that there are three major points of tension that we (conceptually, of course) experience as being in the head, the chest, and the abdomen. I have found that each of these corresponds to particular qualities of experience. And through a gentle investigation and softening – through easing in – we settle in to direct experience more easily and more consistently. Not only that, but it helps to prevent the common over-intellectualization of inquiry by grounding it in the felt experience.

The first point is in the head around the area of the forehead and/or between the eyes. Don't try to find the "correct" point. Rather, just notice if you feel any inner tension in this area. Close your eyes and just sense in this area for a minute or two. When you are done, open your eyes and continue reading.

Next, I'd like you to explore this area again. And this time, notice if there is also a softness or openness there. Not a softness or openness that is opposed to or that negates any tension. Rather, just see if you can tune into a softness or openness that is there. Take a minute or two and do that now with eyes closed, then continue reading when you are ready.

If you were able to tune into a softness or openness there, are you able to also notice that now with eyes open? Take a moment to see if you can tune into the softness with eyes open. Then continue reading.

When you tune into this softness or openness, what else do you notice? What shifts in your experience? Do you notice that your attention also softens and that direct experience is more readily obvious? There is no right or wrong answer here. But just take a moment to observe.

Next, let's explore the second point. The second point is in the chest, most commonly in the area of the sternum. For the next minute or two, with eyes closed, sense this area and just notice if you are aware of any inner tension there. When you are ready, open your eyes and continue reading.

As you did with the first point, explore now to see if you can tune into softness or openness in and around this second point. Take a minute or two to do that now with eyes open or closed and then continue reading when you are done.

The third point is in the lower belly, just below the navel and typically interior to the body. Take a moment to observe if you are aware of any inner tension in this area. And then see if you are also able to tune into any softness or openness. Do that now and then continue reading when you are done.

What I find to be very useful about Somatic Self-inquiry is that it gives a simple and felt means to discover the softness and openness of direct experience. When I feel particularly reactive, this simple form of inquiry gives me a powerful way to quickly ease in to the open, non-reactive wholeness that underlies all experience.

I encourage you to test this out for yourself. Put it to the test in your life. As you are going about your day, whenever you notice you are reactive, just take a moment to tune into the softness and openness at these three points. You may discover, as I do and as do many others who I have shared this with, that this simple process gives quick access to easing in.

The Importance of Frequency

Easing in to direct experience is powerful. You may have already noticed that each time you do this you get immediate access to wholeness and freedom.

But then what happens in the next moment? For most of us, the habit is to re-contract into the habitual reactivity and give our attention to the conceptual overlay. We jump right back into trying to figure out all our problems, winding ourselves up into more and more stress and tension. It is a vicious cycle.

Fortunately, the remedy is always available. In an instant, we can ease in to direct experience. We can notice the softness and openness that is here. And we can allow ourselves to sink beneath the turbulence of the conditioned reactivity.

This gives us the ability to begin to act from choice – to choose to be moved in alignment with our deepest desires and values – as we'll see in the next sections. But we only have access to this when we choose it. And if we only choose it once in a while, we can suffer needlessly the rest of the time.

That is why frequency matters. The more frequently you ease in to direct experience, the more frequently you experience the healing balm of this softness and openness and wholeness. Not only that, but the more it begins to infuse your life. The more it becomes the essence of the new conditioning in your life. This allows you to become less reactive, more patient, more compassionate, more understanding, more loving – not just in your heart of hearts, but in your day to day actions.

Unfortunately, if we are tightly wound up and highly reactive, this can seem difficult at first. But fortunately, we have no shortage of opportunities and reminders to ease in. Every upset, frustration, and reaction is a reminder to ease in.

Apart from using every upset or difficulty as a reminder to ease in, another useful thing is to set an alarm as a reminder to ease in throughout the day. I co-facilitate a training in a similar form of inquiry with a friend of mine. With that program we consistently see huge, sustained shifts for the participants. And one of the key ingredients that I am convinced makes it so profoundly effective for people is that we support people *daily* in applying the simple forms of inquiry in their daily lives many times each day over eight weeks. Many participants in that program use timer apps on their phones to remind them to "access" (i.e. ease in) every half hour or some other frequency throughout the day.

The frequency matters a great deal. The myth that many people continue to believe is that a single glimpse is likely to produce sustained transformation. The reality is that the more frequently you ease in (or access or glimpse or whatever you want to call it), the more rapid and profound and sustained the transformation will be.

Use everything you can to your advantage. Use everything that you can to remind you to ease in, to notice the softness and openness that is here in and as and through all experience.

Living Ease In Life

With many direct inquiry approaches, a common problem that people encounter is that it doesn't translate into real change in their lives. In fact, too often, it turns into a kind of escapism. People discover that there is a peace and freedom available to them, but they mistakenly believe that this peace and freedom is only found inwardly. They don't take the next step that allows this essential discovery to cross over into their lives.

That approach of retreat inwardly may work for renunciates. This may be one reason why in many spiritual traditions the most serious adherents renounce the world and retreat to monasteries or caves.

But you and I are not renunciates. We live in the world. We have bills and responsibilities. I have children who I care for and live with every day. I have relationships with my friends and neighbors.

For you and me and people like us, we need a different way. We need to bring this "inward" discovery into our daily lives. We need to bridge the gap and allow the easing into direct experience to inform and guide our actions, words, and relationships.

Although this presents many challenges, it also presents many opportunities. Even though there are times when I have the thought that I wish it was easier, the deeper truth is that I am daily grateful for the challenges of my life.

That is why the Ease In Method has two parts. First is the easing into direct experience. Second is the flow of ease into life. In other words, we find ease in being then ease in life.

This two-fold path or method is, in my biased opinion, highly rewarding. It dissolves remaining conceptual boundaries between inner and outer. And it facilitates the experience of greater flow in life.

It also continues to soften and humble us.

In the arrogance of youth, softening and humility didn't sound like good things to me. I just wanted power and control. I wanted to protect my self-interests and gain for myself what I thought would help me.

But in the little wisdom that I have gained in my (slight) maturity, I have come to appreciate how valuable softening and humility are. When we consciously participate in this softening and humility through the second step of the Ease In Method, we discover that we are freer than we ever knew and we become more able to connect to and express our authentic desires.

Far from finding that we are depleted and harmed by the challenges of life, we find that all the challenges offer us the gift of discovering how to express what we have always most valued. It reveals the love, compassion, and patience that is at our depths and allows it to flow into expression in our lives.

Importantly, it does not always look the way we thought that it should look. In fact, it rarely looks the way we thought it should look. Because most of the time we thought it had to look like our personalities as perfectly virtuous – always kind, always right, always good.

But what we get to discover instead is the deeper compassion and humility that reveals how we truly are connected. Not through our imaginary perfection, but through the reality of our perfection that appears in all these flawed ways.

It reveals that the real gifts of life are not found in getting it all right. The real gifts are found in the tenderness that shines forth through our seeming flaws...when we are humbled enough to just be ourselves as we are in this moment.

Let's now explore how to allow this direct recognition of wholeness to flow and ease into our lives, to fulfill our truest, most authentic desires.

I'll start with an example from my own life, one that is often front and center for me since my wife and I have three young children who we homeschool. In fact, as I have written the majority of this manuscript, I've done so while standing in the same room with my wife and three children and the apparent chaos that is common in our lives.

My children want what they want, and they don't want anyone telling them no or getting in their way. However, there are many, many times each day in which I say no. I say no to things that I perceive to be dangerous, destructive, or needlessly disruptive. Like when my six-year-old son grabs things from my three-year-old daughter. Or when my three-year-old daughter retaliates by hitting my six-year-old son with a rock. Or when my eight-year-old daughter tries to trick my son into something that feels bad to him like a trade that leaves him feeling ripped off and confused. Or when one of them nearly sets the house on fire. Or when one of them is yelling loudly in my ear. Or any of the other dozens of things that happen every day.

When I say no, regardless of how clearly or nicely I say it or how much I get down to their height and engage with them in a positive way or how much I appeal to their self-interest, this often results in a conflict. Sometimes they ignore me. Sometimes they keep doing whatever I am telling them no about. Sometimes they even yell at me or try to hit or kick me (mostly my three-year-old, not so much the older two).

This has gotten easier for me to experience less reactivity and to have more patience even when I experience reactivity. But I won't lie to you and say that I don't experience a lot of reactivity still. I sometimes feel angry. Sometimes impatient. Sometimes frustrated. Sometimes I just want them to "behave" and to comply with my requests. Sometimes I want to yell.

Sometimes – like the time when my son hit me with a metal pole because he was feeling afraid that I was going to take away some food or something (I don't even remember) that he had hidden behind a log – I actually *do* yell. In that particular instance, I lost my cool entirely. I even held him down while I shouted "don't ever hit me". Not a moment that I feel proud of. But a moment that humbled me and that has taught me even more deeply than I could have understood previously how important it is to me to tune into my most authentic desires and be moved by those rather than reactive impulses.

I live intentionally closely with my children. I intentionally don't seek to retreat to private spaces to get space and quiet. (I only find a private space when offering a meeting space or workshop for others in order to honor their needs for more quiet and privacy.) I make this choice because I value the intimacy and connection I get from being with them.

Intimacy is vulnerable. And in vulnerability I find abundant opportunities to make use of the Ease In Method.

The first step, as we've already explored together, is to discover the underlying wholeness that is already present. This is available to us regardless of circumstance. So whether I am in a quiet, private space and feeling comfortable and good or whether I am in a chaotic, public space feeling uncomfortable and bad, this underlying wholeness is accessible. It is here and it is always closer than anything else, so to speak. It doesn't require effort to find it. In fact, any effort to find it only seems to make it far away. But the moment we ease in to direct experience, we can find it already here.

The second step is to discover in this direct experience of wholeness what the true desire is that is most obvious. This doesn't require analysis or thinking. It arises out of clarity. It is obvious. It is innocent.

I failed to do this in the moment when my son hit me and I reacted by yelling and pinning him to the ground. But what I could have done, had I allowed myself the space is to pause, tune into the wholeness that is here, and then noticed the innocent, authentic desire. I could have then allowed myself to be moved by that authentic desire rather than the reactivity.

That desire, which I can notice right now as I remember the scenario, is for connection. By tuning into that authentic desire and being moved by that rather than reactivity, my action could have been congruent with that desire.

I mention this example of how I "failed" for a few reasons. First, I think it is important to point out that we don't need to hold ourselves to impossible standards. Neither do we need to shame ourselves or hide the fact that we are human and that we sometimes react and do things we wish we could have done differently.

We don't benefit from comparing ourselves to others in a negative way. We aren't other people. We don't have their conditioning and their circumstances. We have our conditioning and our circumstances. We can't be other people. And we definitely can't be our *ideas* about what other people are based on what we see of them.

We benefit from being ourselves. Being honest and vulnerable. When we are willing to simply meet ourselves where we are and as we are, we can have compassion for ourselves. Then we can ease in to direct experience and be moved by our authentic desires. This won't necessarily feel and look like we thought it should. But we can choose to trust that it is perfect as it is, even if our actions and feelings aren't what we consider to be perfect.

Another reason I mention this is because even though we will not be perfect, we can learn even form our mistakes. I learned a lot from that experience. I learned that I can react in ways that are hurtful. That is humbling and gives me access to greater compassion. Rather than being burdened by the need to judge others for similar reactivity, I can recognize that same reactivity within myself and have compassion for them and for myself. We are all human and we are all in this together.

I also point this out because it is never too late to have forgiveness for ourselves or for others. Even though I made that mistake, I get to forgive myself for that and learn from the mistake. I can notice how the space and access to wholeness was there and I just overlooked it in the moment. But in retrospect it is clear that the access to wholeness was present, and in seeing this I get to have greater clarity and I can more readily recognize this wholeness next time I find myself in a situation that is stressful and in which I experience a strong impulse to react in a way that would be hurtful.

Perhaps the most important reason (in my opinion) why I point this out, however, is to make the point that how and whether we allow ourselves to be moved by authentic desires arising from wholeness matters. When inquiry is one-sided and over-intellectualized, it can be used to justify any action or non-action. We can justify it all because "nothing really matters", "nothing exists", "there is no person", "it is all one", "it is only illusion", etc.

Yet as I pointed out earlier, though it is true on one level that there is no flame and no hand, stick your (non-existent) hand in the (non-existent) flame and you'll get burned. The pain of wrong action or of denying our humanity points us to discover how we are lying to ourselves. It encourages us to recognize the larger flow, to discover that wholeness does not deny or reject illusion, objects, people, or anything else. Just because there are no objects outside of concepts doesn't mean that nothing is real. It just means our beliefs about this aren't the same as the reality of this.

This is why I wholeheartedly believe and experience that the second step of the Ease In Method – the step in which we allow our authentic desires arising from wholeness to move us into right action – is so important. It remedies what I think of as the "death cult" of over-intellectualized philosophy by waking us up to our humanity as being non-separate from non-conceptual wholeness. And it allows the inherent ease and peace and fluidity of wholeness to flow into our experience.

Most situations that we encounter in our lives aren't so intense as the one I described above. As such, they don't provoke such strong reactions. Learning from the experiences in which we lose perspective and are reactive – discovering that wholeness is always present – allows us to have greater patience and to more readily ease in to direct experience, pause, and move from our authentic desires in all the less intense experiences.

Now, let me give you a few examples of how the complete, two-step process of the Ease In Method might work. These are both examples from my recent experience.

First, here is an example of how to apply the Ease In Method to manifest what we truly desire, even though that may not look like we thought it should or needed to. This is important because this is often the case.

This morning, my son became upset because he wanted a muffin and despite the fact that my wife was attempting to help him with that, something about it was displeasing to him. Whether it was because it wasn't happening soon enough or because he was afraid that it wouldn't turn out the way he had in mind or for some other reason, I don't know. I don't know because he didn't express that in a way that I was able to understand. All I did understand was that he was upset. And I understood that because he was making loud sounds that I felt a reaction to in my body that was unpleasant to me.

To say "unpleasant" is somewhat of an understatement. It is my observation – and I could be wrong about this – that children seem to have a talent for discovering the sounds and behaviors that are most offensive to their parents or primary caregivers. Maybe not all children, but many children I know seem to have this talent. And my son definitely has figured out how to make the sounds that I find to be very jarring and unsettling.

So when he was expressing his upset in this way, of course I was motivated out of selfishness to help him meet his perceived needs so he could *please stop making that noise.* But my son didn't want to hear anybody. Any attempts to communicate using words only resulted in more noises.

What to do? The Ease In Method is my saving grace in these situations. On the surface I am reactive and feel an urgent desire to change the circumstances. Slightly beneath that I feel powerless and hopeless. Slightly underneath that a rage at this impotence.

Over time I have exhausted the strategies that I know from my conditioning. I've drawn upon what I had modeled for me as a child. I've drawn upon what I've had friends suggest to me. I've drawn upon things I've read in parenting books. And while some of those things are sometimes helpful, there are still many times when all the strategies fail. All I am left with is what is happening.

If I give power to the reactivity, I find myself acting in ways that are not congruent with my true desires. Like the situation I described above when I reacted to my son hitting me. Since that has always felt bad to me, I am motivated to do something different.

Here's how that played out when my son was upset about the muffin and making noises that my body was reacting to. I paused. I observed my experience. And I eased into the direct experience.

What was happening in direct experience? Sound, vibration, energy, contraction, aversion, urgency. Could I know the meaning of this or that I needed to do something about it? No. There was no obvious present danger and also no obvious way to resolve any of it.

So what remained available was to continue to tune into the direct experience. From this easing into wholeness came clarity. The clarity wasn't in words, but the best words I can use to express that clarity are "I desire peace."

At the level of conditioned mind, "peace" means "make the sound stop". But in direct experience, from wholeness, it is clear that peace is not dependent upon the sound stopping. I can choose peace by choosing, first and foremost, to remain aware of this wholeness. In fact, what is clear in this direct inquiry is that this wholeness is peace, and it is from this that peace can be expressed in ways that are congruent.

Next, I can allow this authentic desire for peace and the intimate recognition of this peace that is already present and not dependent upon conditions to move me into action.

In this case, the action was subtle. It was clear that trying to intervene was not going to help express that peace. So what could I do? I could be present.

This is subtle. But it is also something that we all have experience of. We know when someone is present in an open, compassionate, supportive way. In contrast, we know when someone is simply trying to fix something according to their agenda.

To be present in this open way is to not turn away or try to avoid the feelings or experiences that are happening. It is to be available for whatever need presents itself. But it is to continue to ease in to this openness and wholeness without indulging reactivity.

Eventually, my wife and son worked it out. I didn't need to "do" anything.

Here's a second example. Recently my wife and I had a conversation that left me feeling uncomfortable and unsettled. It was not a huge blow out or a call for divorce. But she expressed some feelings that left me feeling vulnerable and unresolved in ways that felt uncomfortable.

On the surface, I thought I wanted her to do certain things in order for me to get the experience that I thought I wanted. I thought that if she would acknowledge me and my contributions to our family, if she would acknowledge my acts of love and support, and if she would show me that she appreciates me in the ways that I could most easily understand, then I would feel better. And I thought that if I could only feel better, that would be what I want.

But since none of that magically happened and since in my attempts to figure it out in my imagination it was clear that all my conditioned reactivity and all my learned strategies would only make things worse...all that was available to me in truth was to just soften and open to the vulnerability and rawness of the direct experience.

Without trying to fix anything, I simply inhabited the direct experience. And from that it was clear that what I most authentically desired was what I could best call connection. To be clear, this was not an analytical process. I didn't do a 10-step worksheet to conclude that my authentic desire is connection. Neither did the recognition of my authentic desire need a word such as connection. But I could sense the authentic desire.

I stayed with that authentic desire. And in this case, it actually required a day of remaining with that without trying to force a resolution or fix anything. It was uncomfortable, but it was all that was available that was true in my experience.

From that came the clarity of action. I was moved by this authentic desire. I realized that I didn't actually have a need for the circumstances to change. I didn't have a need for her to do anything differently. I didn't need her to vocalize her approval of me. I didn't even need her to approve of me. I wanted connection. And that connection is already present and found here in wholeness.

From this, the action was obvious. Let go and act from connection. I approached her, asked her if she wanted to hold one another, and when she responded affirmatively, we held one another and experienced the expression of that authentic desire for connection.

The important point here is that what I might think the conditions are isn't the deeper truth. Had I been waiting for her to behave a particular way or for me to experience a particular feeling state, I could still be waiting. But instead, being moved by that deeper, authentic desire, the connection that is already present came to be expressed and made manifest.

This is very different from how my relationships used to be. Even with my wife, I used to hold on to hurt for days, strategizing and seeking to "punish" by withdrawing. That never gave me what I really wanted, though. So from those experiences I have been given the gift of humility to receive the deeper connection that is already present and to be moved by that.

I am proposing to you that this works in every situation and circumstance. In every relationship. In every condition.

But it only works when we allow it to work. It works when we ease in and allow that ease to manifest by moving us. This appears to be our singular true power: to ease in and allow that ease to move us. Anything else is false power, and false power only causes pain. Even when we get what we think we want, we never get what we truly want when we use the false power to manipulate and strategize. But when we allow this authentic power to move us, we discover a deeper satisfaction.

Part III: Practical Application of the Ease In Method

From my perspective, the Ease In Method is a way of life. It is applicable to any circumstance and every situation. It offers us a direct and immediate way to recognize wholeness, discover our authentic desires, and to be moved into action that is congruent with our authentic desires. It both instantaneously gives us access to healing and peace and it allows us to mature and evolve in our expression of that so that we heal more and more over time.

Our lives become richer and better when we apply this method. At least that is my experience. And I have seen it to be true for others as well.

Although it can be applied to any circumstance and situation, I want to give you some practical examples of how this can be applied to discover healing in a variety of specific conditions. In the following sections, I'll share with you my own experiences of how I have successfully applied the Ease In Method to discover healing in different conditions.

Ease In Method for Anxiety

Anxiety is one of those things that a great many people struggle with. Whether generalized anxiety, social anxiety, or whatever other form of anxiety, many people suffer with anxiety. Because so few of us know how to find healing through anxiety, too many of us have allowed anxiety to result in isolation, shame, and sometimes even poverty, homelessness, drug addiction, and worse.

I experienced a lot of anxiety in my life. Anxiety around people judging my body. Anxiety around smelling bad. Anxiety around making mistakes during performances (I have done a lot of musical performances since a young age). Anxiety around eating. Lots and lots of anxiety.

I would say that anxiety was the underlying basis of many of the other symptoms I struggled with, including some of the others that I'll detail in the following sections. But here, I'd like to explore generalized anxiety. I'll share with you how I have applied the Ease In Method to find healing from this type of anxiety.

I often experienced anxiety that I attributed to circumstances and situations. But there were also times when I could find no obvious explanation for the anxiety. I would be in a safe environment with no obvious stressors and suddenly feel highly anxious. This type of anxiety provides an interesting opportunity because without any obvious causes, a non-anxious person might think that the anxious person could simply "drop it".

But for many years that was certainly not my experience. Instead of dropping it, I would spin around and around in my mind and body trying to fix it. I would try to calm down. I would try to find the cause. I would research all kinds of possible reasons for the anxiety. Once I had broadband internet access, I was able to find online forums and read other people's theories.

The Ease In Method helped me to solve my generalized anxiety problem both instantly and progressively. Here's how I have applied it. Whenever I would feel anxious, I'd pause and observe to see if there was any obvious explanation. Once I started to get out of 24/7 panic mode, I discovered that there were sometimes some obvious explanations that I hadn't previously considered. One major example in my case was that I needed to eat. Not eating enough was a major contributor to anxious feelings for me, but I had never noticed that until I started to apply the Ease In Method consistently.

If I couldn't find any obvious reasons and address them, next I would begin to ease into direct experience. The most obvious way to explore that in my experience was to explore my feelings and sensations in direct experience. I noticed that I had sensations that I perceived to be "fast" and "energetic" and "uncomfortable" throughout my body. Those sensations were what I had come to know as anxiety.

In direct experience it was obvious that I couldn't find anxiety apart from the sensations and some thoughts that I believed were anxious thoughts. So I had to admit that all that I could definitely know was that I seemed to be experiencing these sensations and thoughts. In direct experience these sensations and thoughts were not problems. They were just happening.

Of course, my conditioning was still to react. But I continued to explore in direct experience. By continuing to ease in to direct experience, I started to become curious about these sensations. And what I found time and time again was that the sensations weren't what I had initially thought they were.

Although I had initially thought they were fast, energetic, and uncomfortable, what I found by continuing to explore in direct experience was that they were just sensations happening. I couldn't say for sure what they were other than that. I definitely couldn't be sure that I knew what they meant. And I had to start to admit a deeper truth, which was that these sensations weren't actually harming me.

There wasn't actually a problem! That was surprising to discover. At first, I couldn't believe it. I was so convinced that there must be a problem. But I kept exploring in direct experience and could not find that these sensations actually posed a threat of any kind.

The more I explored in this way, the more it started to become clear that these sensations were just energy. It was my conditioned reactivity that was so unpleasant. Not the sensations themselves.

For me, discovering how to somatically open and soften the impulses to react by tensing up and closing down was very powerful. I started to explore softening and opening, and this allowed me to experience the flow of energy rather than trying to protect myself from it.

From this, I started to notice my authentic desires. My authentic desires in these "generalized anxiety" situations could best be described as communion. I wanted to consciously commune with life. It was as if I was getting a strong signal in the form of intense energy that was alerting me to pause and tune in to wholeness.

I've often pushed myself too hard and kept my nose to the grindstone. I actually did need reminders to take a break and "smell the roses". What a surprise to discover that in my case, generalized anxiety was that reminder to rest in myself and open to wholeness. To consciously open to joy.

Ease In Method for Anorexia

For anyone who has never struggled with anorexia or another type of eating disorder, the solution seems obvious. In the case of anorexia, the "obvious" solution is to eat. In the case of bulimia, the obvious solution is not to purge.

But for anyone who has struggled with eating disorders, we know that the answer isn't that straightforward. Because the behavior – the restricting, the over-eating, the purging – is a symptom, not the cause.

The cause is the avoidance of scary or uncomfortable feelings.

The feelings seem so overwhelming, so terrifying, so unacceptable that the compulsive behaviors seem better. Even if that means starving oneself. Or purging. Or eating way beyond the point of fullness.

In my case, I struggled both with overeating (mostly when younger) and starving myself.

When I struggled with those things, I didn't understand why I was doing it. Not really. I just felt that I had to. But in retrospect it is clear that always, I was trying to avoid unwanted feelings.

When I was younger and would overeat to the point of pain...and then keep eating...I had feelings of pointlessness, hopelessness, and boredom that I was trying to cover up and avoid with eating.

When I was starving myself, I had feelings of being out of control, disgusting, and unlovable that I was trying to cover up and avoid by starving myself.

The feelings were feelings I had in my body. So the words I have used to describe the feelings weren't the feelings themselves. The feelings were feelings. But the words point to a certain "flavor" of feelings.

When I finally "woke up", I began to apply the Ease In Method to my struggles with anorexia. This was one of the most challenging things I applied the Ease In Method to, to be honest. It was considerably harder for me than OCD – and OCD was challenging. The feelings were so strong and my conditioned avoidance was so strong that I was terrified.

Still, it was clear that I didn't want to continue to suffer. So I chose to apply the method. And here's how I did it. First of all, I just told myself the truth any time I was tempted to starve myself. That truth was that starving myself never worked. It never gave me what I really wanted. So I knew that applying the method would be better than what I had been doing.

Then, I would ease into direct experience through the direct exploration of the feelings. In direct experience, I found that I had feelings in my body that I believed were uncomfortable and frightening. But as I continued to explore, I had to admit that these feelings weren't actually harming me. And furthermore, I couldn't know for sure what the feelings meant. So despite the fact that I was conditioned to fear the feelings and believe they meant something bad, I found no proof of that being true in direct experience.

Since I couldn't find any proof that the feelings meant anything bad or that they meant that I should starve myself, I choose to take small steps with eating. I would get a "forbidden food" and I would eat some of it and just be with the feelings in direct experience. I continued to do this persistently over time. And the more I did it, the more I could trust that nothing bad was happening.

As I said, this was quite challenging for me. It took a lot of patience and commitment. But it worked.

Through this, it became clear that my authentic desire was for nourishment – deeply nourishment. I could find this nourishment in wholeness, and I allowed this to spill over into my life. Through direct inquiry I could not find any evidence whatsoever that I am unlovable or that I don't deserve nourishment at a physical level. And so I had to admit that the only sensible thing to do was to live in accordance with that.

Ease In Method for OCD

If you've never struggled with obsessive-compulsive disorder, you might think it is just about being a "neat freak" or some other common misconception. But it is not. It can take over a person's life. The rules, the rigidity, the checking, the intense fear and worry can consume a person.

In my case, I counted everything. I checked everything many times over (making sure I locked the door, making sure the stove was off, making sure I hadn't sent an email to the wrong person, etc.). I washed my hands compulsively. I worried about what every little spec of anything anywhere might be (might be drugs, might be poison, might be...). I felt compelled to do everything the "right" way, but the "right" way was ever-changing. And I never go anything *quite* right. I had "good" words and "bad" words. The rules for my life were eve-changing and impossible for me to get right. It was tortuous.

Even though anorexia was killing me, OCD was more "in my face". OCD dominated my life. From morning to night, I obsessed and did compulsive behaviors. And nothing really helped to relieve that stress.

So curing my OCD problem was a high priority. But it was challenging because the feelings I experienced were so intense.

I did compulsive behaviors because I was terrified of the feelings I had. I was afraid *not* to do the compulsive behaviors because I feared that not doing the compulsive behaviors would further intensify the feelings. (But, of course, the more I indulged the compulsive behaviors, the worse things got. So it was a vicious cycle.)

I had tried to simply avoid the compulsive behavior. But until I discovered the Ease In Method, the only way I had to do that was through suppressing the behavior. Eventually, the intensity of the feelings would grow so great that I would cave in and do the compulsive behavior. I couldn't win through will power alone.

Here's how I applied the Ease In Method. I eased into the direct experience of the feelings. Exploring in direct experience, I could not find any proof that the feelings meant what I had thought they meant (basically, something terrible). And so I continued to explore in this open and curious way.

I also made extensive use of the somatic inquiry – softening and opening the inner tension. This further revealed that the feelings were just energy without any certain meaning. I had to admit that the feelings – the energy – weren't hurting me. It was just energy.

This made it possible for me to discover my most authentic desire. My authentic desire in this case was openness, presence, and freedom to choose. I could see how I had been so conditioned to struggle and fight and try to "win" in life that I hadn't recognized the call to slow down and just be. Through this I discovered that I don't have to "win" or do anything to deserve to be. Whether I "deserve" to be or not, I am. And I gratefully receive that gift moment to moment.

Using the Ease In Method with OCD was certainly challenging, but it worked remarkably well. With persistent application, I not only learned how to ride out intense obsessions and compulsions. I also discovered a deeper desire that spilled over into my life and expresses as actual freedom from obsessions and compulsions. Every once in a while, I still experience some mild obsessions or compulsions under stress. But honestly, having said that, I can't even remember the last time it happened. And when it has happened, I just applied the Ease In Method to discover deeper freedom. My most common experience these days is of freedom and ease in my thinking and feelings. I don't obsess or worry. This has given me a faith in goodness in life. I have positive expectation instead of fearful apprehension.

Ease In Method for Multiple Chemical Sensitivities

I have coached people who have struggled with sensitivities more severe than mine were, but the same approach has worked in each case thus far.

In my case, I experienced relatively mild physical reactions. I experienced burning eyes, aches and pains, itchiness, and most likely some other symptoms that I unable to remember now that it's been so long since I last experienced them.

The truth was that my most significant symptoms were symptoms of panic. I felt that I couldn't breathe. And I was terrified of things getting worse. I was on high alert for every scented product, every possible mold contamination, every off-gassing product, every exposure to exhaust, and on and on.

The fact that I was experiencing panic made it easier for me than some people I've coached to recognize that it really wasn't the scents, the chemicals, or any of the other things that I had focused on for such a long time. I've coached people who have struggled to recognize this, but they eventually do. And when they do, they have all (thus far) recognized that underneath the reactions is intense feeling.

It is definitely possible to inquire into the direct experience of the reactions themselves -t he sensations (the itchiness, the burning, the nausea, etc.). And if all else fails, this would be the place to start. But honestly, it is easier to inquire directly into the feelings that aren't so easily connected to manifest symptoms. What I mean is, if a person has hives or welts or red eyes or sores, this can be more challenging for most people because their minds will usually keep telling them that the manifest symptoms that they can see are "proof" that the condition is caused by chemical exposure. So they can spin round and round (and get nowhere) in suffering.

Whereas, inquiring directly into the inward feelings of anxiety or buzzing or intensity or panic (or whatever words a person uses to describe their inner experience) is typically going to be much more productive.

In my case, I inquired directly into the inner feelings of panic and discovered that in direct experience the feeling wasn't harming me and I had no proof that it was bad or a problem. I continued to inquire and discovered that actually, in direct experience, it was just energy that had no boundaries. And truthfully, it could just as well be called excitement or pure energy or any number of other things.

I then discovered, through somatic inquiry, how I was contracting and trying to protect myself against the feelings. This led to hyperventilation that reinforced the feelings of panic. It was a vicious cycle. But through this direct inquiry, I saw it for what it was. And I then began to explore softening and opening.

At first it was challenging because my mind was so wound up and wanted to make a problem out of everything. Everything felt like a threat. But through direct inquiry and the commitment to soften and open (letting my breathing relax helped too), I started to discover that nothing was really happening that I needed to be concerned about.

It is important to understand (I think so, at least) that the nose has a more direct connection to the emotional center of the brain than do the other sense organs. As such, it is quite natural that scents can provoke a rapid emotional reaction – faster than anything else. Knowing this, I found it was possible to just remember that my reactions were due to conditioning that was too fast for my normal consciousness to intervene in. But through continuing to inquire, I trusted that I was slowly changing that conditioning.

Sure enough, it worked. And I've seen it work for others I've coached in this process as well. It just requires persistent application.

In terms of what authentic desires came to light in the process, what I discovered was that underlying it all was an authentic desire for okayness. Of course, that is probably obvious once I point it out. After all, all fear is actually expressing an authentic desire for okayness. Yet through easing into direct experience it is possible to discover the source of okayness that is always present – even when there are intense feelings, including panic. Continuing to ease into this okayness and let it inform my actions, I chose to soften and open...as if I was already okay (because I recognized that I was even though I had intense feelings at the same time). This resulted in progressively experiencing greater ease and feelings that I could more easily recognize as okayness.

Ease In Method for Chronic Fatigue

One of the things I didn't really mention in my story in the first part of this book was about my struggles with chronic fatigue. Despite all my severe treatment of my body, I had quite a lot of energy until I was about 26 years old. When I lived in California I practiced yoga every day for one to two hours, lifted weights three or four times each week, and hiked daily. But when I moved to Boston, Massachusetts, I suddenly couldn't make it through a single yoga class due to fatigue.

For years I attributed this to mold exposure. When I first moved to Boston my apartment flooded three times in the first month. And so I had a story in my mind that told me that the flooding caused mold growth that led to chronic fatigue.

Over the years, it grew worse, becoming so severe after my experiences with Lyme disease that I struggled even to have the energy to stand up.

At that point I had the story that not only had I been poisoned by mold exposure, I was also infected with "chronic Lyme disease". I had fears that the mold and the bacteria were destroying me from the inside.

What I've discovered in the years since was that the chronic fatigue was primarily due to the chronic (physical and psychological) armoring and expenditure of energy trying desperately to protect myself psychologically and emotionally.

It took me a number of years of applying the Ease In Method before I finally discovered true healing from chronic fatigue. I am happy to report to you that I no longer struggle with chronic fatigue, however.

Here's how I applied the Ease In Method for chronic fatigue. First of all, I had to slow down and notice that every time I was fatigued, I was believing an unhelpful story rather than easing into the direct experience. The essence of the unhelpful story was always that "I'm experiencing fatigue (and it's happening to me)." Or, put another way, "I'm experiencing fatigue and that's a problem."

When I was letting that unhelpful story go unquestioned, I was continuing to run the same programs unconsciously. It was a self-fulfilling prophecy.

So instead, every time I was experiencing what I thought was fatigue, I started to use that as a reminder to ease into the direct experience. In direct experience I couldn't verify that the story was true. Maybe it was true that I was experiencing fatigue – at least on the surface – but I couldn't find evidence in direct experience that it was being done to me, that I was a victim, that it was a problem, or that I needed to do anything about it.

So instead of trying to fix it or fight it or resign myself to it, another possibility became clear: explore my direct experience more. And what I found was that I was in the habit of expending a lot of energy tensing up, contracting, armoring, thinking, searching, and trying to fix my supposed problems (chronic fatigue included). This gave me a lot more to explore in direct experience, and the more I did, the more I discovered how unnecessary so much of it was.

I didn't find any problems in direct experience, and certainly nothing that I needed to protect myself again or armor myself against. And so I began to explore softening and releasing those habits. Again, the somatic exploration was very helpful.

Bit by bit, what started to happen was that I found that the softer I was, the more yielding to my own experience, the more energy I started to discover. My sleep improved. My digestion improved. My relationships improved. All the ways I was struggling from being too wound up and fixated on trying to solve problems simply eased up.

In my own case, I have found that continued somatic exploration has made a huge difference in further releasing these old patterns and habits. As I continue to explore somatically, my body and mind and life ease up and soften.

Using the Ease In Method to Heal Others

One of the amazing things about the Ease In Method is that it is not just for our own healing. We can actually use this approach to help others heal.

I've coached hundreds of people one on one over the past seven years, and I've found that this approach works really well. The biggest mistake I've made and that I believe others often make that prevents this method from working is in failing to actually apply the method. It is sometimes tempting to think that the method can't work to heal others. It can sometimes seem that others have real problems that need to be solved through intervention. But when we are distracted by these thoughts and reactions, we aren't applying the method.

When I see someone through my conditioning, I may not be recognizing their inherent wholeness and perfection. But when I ease into direct experience, I can instantly recognize the wholeness and perfection that is already present.

This is exactly the same as when I apply the method for myself or when you apply the method for yourself. Even though our conditioned interpretation of our circumstances and experiences doesn't necessarily change instantly, we can ease in to direct experience and discover unconditioned wholeness and perfection.

In other words, we may still have the same feelings, same thoughts, same emotions, and same reactivity. But when we ease into direct experience, we perceive it in an unconditioned way. We can do the same for others. Without trying to get rid of our opinions, thoughts, and reactions as they regard others, we can ease into direct experience and perceive their inherent wholeness that doesn't depend on our conditioning. We can feel aversive or fearful feelings and have negative judgments and *still* at the same time we can ease into direct experience and perceive the unconditioned wholeness that doesn't depend on feelings or thoughts that we have come to think of as the feelings and thoughts of wholeness.

In the simplest terms, this is just about being truly present. And it is true non-judgment. Even though we may continue to have judgmental thoughts and opinions, when we perceive these in direct experience, we don't actually *believe* them. This allows us to be present, non-judgmental, and non-reactive...even if we still feel lots of things and have reactive impulses.

Thus far, everyone seems to respond positively to this. Sometimes people respond with confusion or frustration when I am not quick to react and judge them as they are accustomed to. But in the bigger picture, seeing people's inherent wholeness and perfection through direct experience appears to have positive effects.

It seems to offer space to be and space to feel their feelings. It allows for processing to occur – something we typically don't have enough space for when we're feeling under pressure to get things right. And this seems to allow for clarity to arise naturally in a person's experience. The simpler and better solutions to their perceived problems tend to arise. Usually, this helps people to discover that their problems aren't the problems they thought they were.

I have made the mistake many times of telling people how they "should" see things. But that rarely if ever works. In fact, it is only the people who are already quite enlightened who are able to receive such communication in a positive way. My wife surprises me often with her ability to do this. (She's far better at it than I am!)

My experience has shown me that people seem to have had too many lectures from well-intentioned people about how they "should" see things and how they "should" do things. And I am grateful that I have been humbled enough and softened enough that I am able to remember this much of the time now.

When I do remember, I apply the Ease In Method to heal others simply by seeing their wholeness. In seeing their wholeness, I naturally act from this clarity. Someone who is whole doesn't need to fix themselves. They already are whole and have access to that. When I see that and act from that, it gives them the space to naturally recognize that for themselves. No lecturing required!

Conclusion

In this little book I've shared with you what I believe is truly big, big healing. To me, this is true healing – the recognition of wholeness and the expression of that wholeness in our manifest lives.

This is not a "get rich quick scheme" form of healing. It's not the kind of thing that you're going to merely read a book and instantly everything will look and feel the way you think it should.

It is better than that. Whereas the promise of the feelings and experiences that we *think* we want can be alluring, it has never truly satisfied us. And that's because we long for something deeper, something more authentic.

We long to recognize and express the wholeness that we know deep in our heart of hearts to be true.

To get the benefits of the Ease In Method, you have to apply it. When you do, I sincerely believe that you will receive the benefits both instantaneously and progressively. Immediately you can discover everpresent wholeness. And progressively, you can allow this repeated discovery to transform your manifest life.

When you do, I am convinced that you will find, as I have, that you are more satisfied than you had ever imagined possible. Not because you'll have gotten rid of all challenges, difficulties, and unpleasantness. Rather, because you'll know the secret to discovering the gifts in all experiences.

You'll discover that your life is not for you alone. Your gifts are to be shared. And your gifts often show up in the ways you least expect, in the forms you had thought were your weaknesses and shameful qualities. But when you ease in to direct experience and trust in the wholeness that is inherent within you, you will discover that everything about you is in service to this wholeness. Your healing allows you to share the gift of yourself and touch upon countless others.

You don't have to become a teacher or an author to share your gifts. You being you is all that is needed. You already are a gift. I honor you. I thank you. We truly are all in this together.

Many blessings to you.

If you'd like to continue this conversation, I invite you to go to http://joeylott.com/eim

Addendum: Additional Support

Now that we've covered the basics of the Ease In Method as well as seen some practical applications of it, I'd like to share with you some additional things that I have found work really well together with the Ease In Method.

Visualization/Energy Exercises

My experience of the Ease In Method is that it allows for a release of conditioning. Often, as this conditioning is releasing, it results in experiences such as thoughts, memories, feelings, and sensations. Some of these seem to be connected to past experiences that were scary, confusing, unpleasant, infuriating, sad, or traumatic. As such, our typical reaction is to try to stop or avoid these experiences. We may view these experiences as bad or indications that something is going wrong.

Yet time and time again I find that the sooner I allow these experiences to come and go – to flow – the faster my perception of my experience smooths out and I "feel good".

The most obvious solution to this is to continue to apply the Ease In Method. And if that works well for you, great. In that case, nothing else is needed.

But I've also found that some "visualization" exercises can be highly supportive of this. So if you find yourself getting caught up in reacting to your experiences, you may want to explore the following simple exercises.

The River/The Waterfall

When I first started sharing publicly, I created an online program called Peaceful Possibility. In that program I shared a bunch of these kinds of visualization exercises, and among them was one called The Waterfall, which I think is a really nice one, so I'll share it with you here.

The exercise is straightforward. With eyes open or closed, imagine that you are standing under a waterfall of light. Feel the light pouring down on your head and running down, over, and through your body, then seeping deep into the ground. Feel as this light gently warms, loosens, and eases your body from head to toe. It gently carries the experiences with it as it seeps into the ground. Just as a nice shower can help you to feel cleansed not only externally, but energetically, this exercise can help to facilitate the flow of experiences. As you do it, simply let all the experiences come and go in the flow of the waterfall.

Another variation on The Waterfall is The River. The main difference is simply orientation. Whereas the light/energy pours from above with The Waterfall, The River involves the light/energy flowing from the front of the body, through the body.

You can do The River with eyes open or closed. Imagine that you are standing or sitting (or lying down) in a "river" of light. The light flows gently from in front of you and passes over you and through you. As it does, it warms, loosens, and eases your body and carries your experiences in its flow. There is nothing to grasp. Just let it carry everything gently and feel supported and nurtured.

Big Sink

The Big Sink is another exercise from Peaceful Possibility. To do this exercise, feel the part of your body that is in contact with the floor, ground, or other surface that is supporting you. If you are standing, this would be your feet. If you are sitting with feet on the floor, this is your feet. If you are sitting cross-legged, your buttocks are the point of contact. If you are lying down, the part of your body that is making contact with the surface is the point of contact.

Allow yourself to soften and feel that the Earth is pulling gently. Allow yourself to sink. Feel yourself sinking into the Earth as if you were filled with energy that is flowing into the Earth. You are continually nourished and replenished by energy and flow that comes from all around you. And you can simply let yourself continue to let this energy sink into the Earth.

The Earth is fed by our "waste". Our food scraps turn to soil, for example, when we allow them to compost. And in the same way, we can allow our "negative energy" or "waste" flow and sink into the Earth to feed the Earth. The Earth transforms it into positive energy that is released into the environment that can continue to feed us.

Radiant Sun

The Radiant Sun exercise is a new exercise I've recently developed. I really like this one. And it works really well with the Ease In Method because it helps to dissolve the perception of boundaries between inner and outer and reveal wholeness.

Here's how to do the Radiant Sun. With eyes open or closed, visualize or imagine a sun in the center of your chest. This sun is made of light. It is only light. And it radiates light in all directions. Soften and continue to imagine this light radiating in all directions, shining this light on all experiences. As it does, the light reveals all experiences to also be only light.

Somatics

I'm a believer in the power of somatics exploration. I shared with you in Part II a very simple introduction to using somatics with inquiry as part of the Ease In Method. But that is just the tip of the iceberg.

In some sense, qi gong may be one of the longest-standing and most sophisticated systems of somatics work. It is possible – likely, even – that some forms of yoga are based upon the work of yogis who understood somatics deeply (though almost none of the currently-popular forms of yoga are based upon a good understanding of somatics).

But the modern field of somatics can be traced back to the work of Moshe Feldenkrais, who developed a system of healing done through movement-aided awareness cultivation. (There are other contributors to the field of somatics who pre-date Feldenkrais. Frederick Matthias Alexander, the developer of the Alexander Technique is one such example. But Feldenkrais has had a very large influence far beyond anyone else I can think of.) One of Feldenkrais's first American students, Thomas Hanna, further developed this system with his important insights regarding a phenomenon called pandiculation.

Peter Levine developed a system called Somatic Experiencing in recent decades that draws upon some of the same insights, but that was influenced primarily on a different insight he had observing wild animals. I am not as familiar with Somatic Experiencing as I am with other forms of somatics to be able to comment on it, but I make mention of Somatic Experiencing simply because Levine's contributions have had a significant impact on the broader field of somatics.

I have tremendous respect for the contributions of Feldenkrais and Hanna. And certainly, there may be some Clinical Somatic Education instructors (Clinical Somatic Education is the name given to Hanna's somatics work after his death) who have a good understanding of how to make use of that body of work to help people who are severely ill and physical armored. However, it was my experience that I was unable to find real relief or benefits from the Feldenkrais Method or Clinical Somatic Education (from the instructors I learned from). I attribute this to the fact that I was so ill and armored that the explorations they offered were too complex for me to make use of at that time. (Since then, as I've opened and softened, I've found their exercises to be wonderful. But they were inaccessible to me then.)

I have developed my own training in somatics that I call Somatic Re-awakening and Integration. I am deeply grateful to the first group of participants in this training. It is only because of their patience and persistence and their wonderful feedback that I have been able to refine the process to the point it is at today. In retrospect, my initial attempts to communicate the approach were not good. But with the continued feedback, I've been able to develop a simple, gentle, accessible system of movement-aided explorations that develop somatic awareness.

The result is greater ease in the body and mind.

Th premise of somatics – and certainly this is the case with Somatic Re-awakening and Integration – is that when we struggle with feelings of pain, discomfort, or restriction, this is due to conditioning. Thomas Hanna coined a term for this: Sensory Motor Amnesia. We have forgotten how to correctly interpret or understand our sensations and inner experiences. And we have also lost awareness to voluntarily control our bodies in efficient, easeful, pleasurable ways.

As a result, most of our attempts to "fix" the problem are doomed to fail. Not only that, because they don't address the actual cause, they make matters worse because they are compensations that compound the existing conditioning.

With a correct understanding and the correct movement explorations done slowly with awareness, we can quickly restore proper ease and pleasure.

This work is a wonderful complement to the Ease In Method. And I encourage anyone and everyone who experiences chronic pain, discomfort, or restriction; headaches; digestive complaints; insomnia; anxiety; "bad knees"; "bad back"; or "bad anything" to explore this work.

I am biased, of course. I think that Somatic Re-awakening and Integration is amazing, and I would like everyone to check it out. But if you find you are more attracted to other forms of somatics such as those I have mentioned earlier in this section, please feel free to check those out as well.

For anyone who is interested in learning more about Somatic Re-awakening and Integration, I have put together a free introduction to the work that you can get at http://joeylott.com/somatics

Non-Violent Communication & Relationships

Relationships are a wonderful opportunity to deepen in the Ease In Method. The good news is that relationships are unavoidable. (The "bad" news [what sometimes seems like bad news, that is] is that relationships are unavoidable!) Even if we try to isolate, we still have relationships. We are in relationship not only with other humans, but also with everything and also with ourselves.

The Ease In Method can help us to have a radically different relationship with relationship. Rather than having relationship based on conditioned reactivity, we can have relationship based on the recognition of wholeness. This gives us the space to respond rather than react.

What I've found is that skillful means of responding is a huge benefit in relationship. Because I was so conditioned to be reactive, judgmental, fearful, greedy, unkind, inconsiderate, and so forth, I have found it very helpful to admit that my old ways of relating aren't skillful. They don't get me what I want. They don't express what I really want.

Next, using a skillful framework for communicating and relating has proven to be life-changing for me and for those around me who make use of it. There are surely many frameworks for relating that can be effective. The framework that I am familiar with and find to be very useful is called Non-Violent Communication (NVC).

I am not an expert on all the intricacies of NVC. But I have found the rudimentary framework to be very powerful and also very easy to remember. If you want a more in-depth understanding of Non-Violent Communication, I recommend the book by the same name by Marshall Rosenberg. Here I'd like to share with you my understanding of the rudimentary framework and how I find it to be powerful and very supportive and synergistic with the Ease In Method.

NVC as a framework consists of four parts:

1. Observation

2. Feeling

3. Need

4. Request

Let me elaborate on each of these.

Observation refers to observing what is happening or has happened. I've had it described to me by a friend as "the objective data: what a video camera could capture". In other words, in this part we're interested in seeing things without the baggage of our conditioning.

Let's consider an example to make this easier to understand. You'll recall that I described earlier in this book a situation that happened in which my six-year-old son hit me with a metal pole. I reacted in a way that was sad to me (and to him). In this situation, I reacted quickly based on my conditioned interpretation of what happened.

Using NVC, I could have paused and simply observed, perhaps stating my observation out loud (or perhaps not) as, "I think that you just hit me with the metal pole that you're holding."

That's an observation of the facts as I best understood them. In this observation I intentionally want to avoid indulging in judgments or interpretations such as "you hit me with that pole to hurt me" or "you were trying to disrespect me" because I don't actually know that those are true. What is true in that situation is that I am pretty sure that he hit me with the pole.

Next is the feeling part. In this part I want to identify how I feel or felt. In this example could have said, "when that happened, I felt surprised and then I started to feel angry".

Importantly, with NVC we want to take responsibility for having our feelings. That doesn't mean we are to *blame* for our feelings or that we need to fix them. It just means being honest that our feelings are our feelings and that nobody else *causes* our feelings.

You might notice that I wrote "what that happened..." That is fine because I'm just providing context. I'm not blaming anyone for my feelings. That is very different than saying, "you made me angry", because that wouldn't be true. Nobody can make us anything. We might react when people push our buttons. But our reactions are still ours. They arise from within us, whether we like that or not.

The next part is needs. For me, this is intimately connected to the second part of the Ease In Method in which we connect to our authentic desires. Our needs are not simply wants. I don't *need* someone to respect me. What I *need* is love, connection, and okayness. And those are things that someone else can't give me. I have to discover those within myself. In the Ease In Method, I propose that we can find these in our direct experience of wholeness.

In this example, I might say, "My connection with you is very important to me." We don't always have to state our needs. And sometimes it doesn't make as much sense to try to. But other times it is really helpful. I find it helpful with my kids to state these things out loud. It is really helpful for me to actually connect to my authentic needs/desires that arise from wholeness and to state them. When I'm having conflicts with my kids, I find it really helpful to say things such as "I love you and want to support you the best way I can". This is reassuring to both of us...as long as I really am speaking from an authentic desire.

The fourth part is request. This is where we state any request we may have that could help us to move toward a better expression of that authentic desire/need. As I've said, that need is not something anyone can give us, but we most certainly can work together with others in relationship to *express* it more clearly.

In this scenario I might have said, "Would you be willing to tell me what you're needing right now?"

As I have said, this is just the rudimentary framework of NVC. For a more detailed description of NVC, I recommend the book by the same name by Marshall Rosenberg.

Hopefully it is already clear how NVC can work hand-in-hand with the Ease In Method. But let me elaborate. One of the challenges (and benefits) of NVC is that it requires the humility to apply it. If we are highly reactive, we may find it difficult to pause and give ourselves the few seconds of space needed to apply NVC.

It is my experience that practicing the Ease In Method in all aspects of our lives – easing in to direct experience and letting the wholeness we find guide us in our actions – helps to cultivate that space and humility. That makes it much, much easier to apply NVC.

At the same time, NVC gives a framework for expressing our authentic desires, particularly in charged and difficult situations. This helps us to continue to apply the Ease In Method even when things might be the hardest.

I also intend to hold a workshop series on the subject of NVC and the Ease In Method. You can learn more by going to http://joeylott.com/nvc

Nature and Wilderness Immersion

Everything is nature. You and I are nature. Yet the constructs of modern human civilization express a very specific subset of nature. As such, when we spend most of our time within houses, cars, stores, and other human-constructed buildings, we can cut ourselves off from the fullness and wildness of nature.

For this reason, I find that choosing to get outside and immerse ourselves in the wildness of nature can be a powerfully supportive healing practice.

If you live in a big city, it may seem that the wildness of nature is far off. And while it is true that the wildness of nature in big cities is not the most obvious, most dominant feature, it does exist even in big cities. The birds and insects are in the cities too. There are wild plants that grow up between the cracks. There are parks that (no matter how cultivated) still have some of the wildness of nature in them.

If you live in a smaller city or a town, the wildness of nature may be more readily apparent, of course. But wherever you live, simply stepping outside can help you to more easily observe the wildness of nature.

Go for a walk. Open your eyes, and you'll see what you'll see. The cat waiting to pounce on the insect or bird. The bird eating the insect. The insect eating the leaves. The dandelion reaching toward the sun. The plant withering and turning brown as it is shaded out by some other plant. The tree breaking the pavement with its roots. Another tree with cankers on its bark, infected by a virus or bacteria.

Look at the sky and see the clouds. When it rains, feel the rain. When it is dry, feel the dryness.

What is the benefit of this? I am sure there are many benefits. Humans have evolved in the wildness of nature, and being outside connects us to that and gives us direct access to the light, the breeze, the temperature fluctuations, and all the rest of it that our evolution has us expecting.

But what seems to be the most consciously accessible for us is the symbolism of the wildness of nature. It reflects to us the wildness within ourselves. It reflects to us the greater wholeness that – though beyond our conscious understanding, perhaps – is order in chaos, holding it all, allowing it all.

When we are afraid or when we are impatient or when we are angry, we are not trusting this wholeness. We are thinking that our conditioned ideas are right and that wholeness that gives rise to all of life – that has held and nurtured life for all time – is wrong.

The external wildness of nature reflects to us that there is something far greater than our ideas that is already holding it all perfectly. When the robin is eating the worm, there is simply wholeness happening. If I give my attention to the conditioned mind, maybe I will try to figure out what is right. Should the robin eat the worm, knowing the worm must die to feed the robin? Or should the robin forego the worm meal to spare the worm's life? Is the worm more important than the robin or the robin more important than the worm? Who deserves to live and who deserves to die? Is death an injustice? Why does death exist?

These are the kinds of endless questions I can puzzle over at the level of conditioned mind. But in the direct perception of the wildness of nature, the robin is eating the worm. There is no moral overlay needed. There is simply the wholeness and perfection of this moment that does not depend on right and wrong, winning and losing, good and bad.

Sometimes the rain falls in time and the plant survives. Sometimes the rain doesn't fall in time and the plant dies. When the winter comes, the plant may die. Some babies survive. Some do not.

The human conditioned mind calls it a dog-eat-dog world or views the wildness of nature as cruel. This is the conditioned mind that views me as separate from you and bound in time and space. From this perspective, I should not die. From this perspective, my death is the end. And from this perspective, my life is only for me.

But when I see the wildness of nature and simply open to the direct perception of it as it is right now, it reflects to me that this is also my nature. This is what I am. I am not separate from this.

Just as the bird and the sapling are conditioned to try to survive, so too am I conditioned to try to survive. This is healthy and good. Yet nature reveals that everything that has a beginning has an end. But if I carefully observe, I can see that these beginnings and ends are constructs of the mind that seek to separate. The actual observable reality beyond conditioned mind is that there is just this happening. Form changing. One life happening.

This is wholeness. I am this same wholeness. What I can directly discover inwardly is also reflected to me outwardly. In the wildness of nature, I discover this clearly.

I also happen to believe that wilderness immersion beyond simply talking a walk outside on a "nice" day has potential benefits. We don't need to push ourselves to the limits by going alone into the wilderness naked and trying to survive. But to gently explore our conditioned boundaries of comfort in wild places can be very liberating.

Of course, there are genuine dangers found in the wilderness. I had a friend who went to the wilderness of Alaska on his own who never came back. The best guess of those who investigated is that he was killed by a grizzly bear when he returned to the site of where he'd killed a moose the day before.

So I'm not advising anyone to do that. But what I am suggesting is that we all have conditioned boundaries that come up well before the point of facing a grizzly bear alone in the wilderness of Alaska. Most of us don't want to go for a walk outside if it is a little too cold or if it is raining. We can gently explore these boundaries and open to new possibilities. "Maybe I could go for a walk in the rain without suiting up," is a new possibility we could explore, for example.

Myth and Story

Some brands of spirituality denigrate stories. That is, they propose that anything that is "mere story" is a problem.

Certainly it is true that when we don't know how to ease into direct experience and recognize ever-present wholeness – when all we know as reality is our stories about our experiences – this kind of fixation on the stories of our lives can be deeply painful.

But once we know how to ease into direct experience, I propose that it is no longer useful to try to disregard or devalue our stories. Instead, I find that inviting and welcoming our stories as a means to discover the expansion of wholeness within our lives can be quite wonderful.

Myth has long provided value to cultures around the world. And it continues to offer us that same value...when we receive it. Myth provides us with a map to understand the stories of our own lives and the gifts they offer us.

In myth we have a way to recognize how the apparent problems are actually opportunities to discover gifts and for life to expand. When Dorothy (in the Wizard of Oz) begins her story, she is unhappy with her life on the farm in Kansas. This unhappiness is actually revealing a deeper, authentic desire for true happiness or a true home. In order to discover the manifestation of this deeper desire, she goes on a mythical journey to the land of Oz where she has to face the Wicked Witch of the West and discover her gifts.

When we can see our own lives in this light, we can discover how everything is offering us the opportunity to manifest our deepest, most authentic desires. That includes the seeming problems and conflicts in our lives.

Self-Love

Some brands of spirituality propose that "there is no self" as a solution to all perceived problems. From this perspective, it is offensive to consider that self-love would have any value.

But on the other hand, if the default programming is self-hatred, it's not hard to see how that's likely to be unpleasant. And, unfortunately, the "there is no self" brand of spirituality tends to feed into existing patterns of self-hatred, only making things worse.

The truth is, by easing into direct experience, we can easily discover that there is no findable separate self. There is only wholeness, which is inclusive. But at the same time, there remains a *sense* of self. This sense of self is quite functional. It is useful to be able to respond to your name and know when *you* are hungry or tired.

Many of us have a conditioned self-hatred. We learned to reject aspects of ourselves and judge them as disgusting, bad, wrong, or shameful.

That is not an integrated way to live. That is, by definition, disintegrated. And I is unpleasant.

Self-love naturally arises as we allow for an integration of our experience through the consistent application of the Ease In Method. And we can encourage this process further by actively encouraging self-love.

Authentic self-love is not the result of liking or approving of everything about how we behave, think, and feel. That is an old and painful definition of self-love. It is painful because we can never live up to our ideal version of how we should behave, think, and feel.

Authentic self-love is radical self-acceptance. It is allowing and receiving all aspects of ourselves in compassion and clarity. Seeing our behavior, thoughts, and feelings as functions of our conditioning helps us to take it all less personally. From direct experience is it not difficult to see that all of this that we thought of as ourselves is really happening from our conditioning.

When we invest energy rejecting our conditioning, we only perpetuate it. When we receive it all with compassion, we give space for healing – for the manifestation of our authentic desires.

Seeing our conditioning as parts of ourselves that were fragmented at earlier times in our lives can be quite useful. In some respects, this is what actually happened. These thoughts, behaviors, and feelings that we experienced at some earlier point in our lives got rejected by others and ultimately by us. They were then fragmented and we've worked hard ever since to keep them disintegrated.

By seeing the innocence by which these came about in the first place, we can give space for them to be integrated. We often fear that if we view these fragments with compassion, we will be condoning what we don't want. But it is actually just the opposite. By rejecting these fragments, we perpetuate the conditioning. By making compassionate space and allowing integration, we free ourselves from that conditioning.

Final Words

Thank you again for taking the time to read this book. Why am I thanking you? Because we're all in this together. Your healing and my healing are one healing. One wholeness. One wholeness expressing. And when you choose to prioritize your healing, you are shining the light of that wholeness into this world, making it a better place.

Better might be subjective. But subjectively, I think you and I can agree that expressing authentic love, peace, compassion, and joy is good. And your courage to show up fully in this life from and as the wholeness that you know yourself to be in your clearest moments is a gift to the world. A gift to me. And that is why I thank you.

Remember that the Ease In Method works...when you apply it. Whenever you are in doubt, apply the Ease In Method. It works. It helps to reveal greater clarity and greater light even where it seems there is only darkness. It sometimes takes great faith and courage. But the "little miracles" that you can experience applying the Ease In Method grow your faith and courage so you can continue to apply it in your greatest challenges. It is in the greatest difficulties that we discover the greatest light.

And please remember that we truly are in this together. Let's stay in touch. Please visit http://joeylott.com/eim so we can continue the conversation.

CPSIA information can be obtained
at www.ICGtesting.com
Printed in the USA
LVHW091158111119
636960LV00009B/3835/P